KU-466-979

TAXATION SIMPLIFIED
2014-2015

Tony Jones ATT

2000

LEISURE AND CULTURE DUNDEE	
C00734451X	
Bertrams	28/10/2014
	£14.99
REF	336.20094

Copyright © Management Books 2000 Ltd 2014

All rights reserved. No part of this publication may be reproduced, stored in a retrieval system, or transmitted in any form or by any means, electronic, mechanical, photocopying, recording, or otherwise without the prior permission of the publishers.

First published in 2014 by Management Books 2000 Ltd
36 Western Road
Oxford OX1 4LG, UK
Tel: 0044 (0) 1865 600738
E-mail: info@mb2000.com
Web: www.mb2000.com

This book is sold subject to the condition that it shall not, by way of trade or otherwise, be lent, resold, hired out, or otherwise circulated without the publisher's prior consent in any form of binding or cover other than that in which it is published and without a similar condition including this condition being imposed upon the subsequent purchaser.

British Library Cataloguing in Publication Data is available

ISBN 9781852527372

Contents

Summary of Rates and Allowances... 9
   A. Rates of Tax... 9
   B. Personal Allowances 10
   C. Tax Credits 10
   D. National Insurance 11

1 The Tax System.. 12
   1.1 Why we need to understand the system 12
   1.2 Why taxes are necessary.. 12
   1.3 Liability to tax.. 13
   1.4 Tax returns.. 13
   1.5 Services from HM Revenue and Customs 14
   1.6 Minimising your tax... 14
   1.7 Providing for payment 16
   1.8 The administration of the system 18
   1.9 The categories of tax... 21
   1.10 The schedular system of direct taxation........................... 23

2 Personal Taxation 24
   2.1 Assessing the liability 24
   2.2 Self-Assessment 25
   2.3 Minimising the liability... 25
   2.4 Specimen computations... 26
   2.5 Reliefs and allowances.. 28
   2.6 Children 30
   2.7 Husband and wife.. 35
   2.8 Salaries, wages and directors' feed..................................... 36
   2.9 Taxable benefits 40
   2.10 Liability insurance and uninsured liabilities 47
   2.11 Life assurance 47
   2.12 National Insurance and Social Security............................... 48
   2.13 Charitable giving... 50
   2.14 Interest paid and home loans 51
   2.15 Making provision for retirement 52

3 Savings Income 56
   3.1 A summary of the system... 56
   3.2 Personal Equity Plans (PEPs).. 58
   3.3 Interest receivable... 59
   3.4 Individual Savings Accounts (ISAs)...................................... 61
   3.5 Profit sharing 62

3.6   Enterprise Investment Scheme (EIS) 65
3.7   Venture capital trusts 66
3.8   Scrip dividends 66
3.9   Unit trusts 66
3.10   Offshore funds 67
3.11   Seed Enterprise Investment Scheme 67
3.12   Social Investment Relief 68

4   **Business Taxation** 69
4.1   The system summarised 69
4.2   Adjusting the accounts profit 70
4.3   A specimen computation 74
4.4   Capital allowances 77
4.5   Turnover under £81,000 87
4.6   Unincorporated businesses/partnerships 88
4.7   Relief for losses 89
4.8   Companies and corporation tax 90
4.9   Investment companies and close companies 94
4.10   Self-employed persons 95
4.11   Withholding tax 99

5   **Capital Gains** 100
5.1   General nature of the tax 100
5.2   Rates of tax 101
5.3   The principal exceptions 101
5.4   Calculating the gain 102
5.5   Entrepreneurs' relief 105
5.6   Trustees 106
5.7   Losses 106
5.8   Replacement of assets (rollover relief) 107
5.9   Death of the tax-payer 108
5.10   Payment of tax 108
5.11   Sale of private house 108
5.12   Spouses and civil partners 109
5.13   Gifts 109
5.14   Company leaving group 110
5.15   Reinvestment in EIS shares 110
5.16   Bed and breakfasting 111

6   **Rents from Property** 112
6.1   General 112
6.2   Unfurnished and furnished lettings 112
6.3   Furnished holiday lettings 114
6.4   Rent a room scheme 115
6.5   Overseas property 115

7 Miscellaneous Matters **116**
7.1 Additional assessments................................. 116
7.2 Clubs and societies 116
7.3 The Council Tax.. 117
7.4 Error or mistake.. 119
7.5 Income from abroad 120
7.6 Interest on tax.. 127
7.7 Discretionary and accumulation trusts 127
7.8 Visitors to the UK.. 128
7.9 Stamp duty 128

8 Value Added Tax **130**
8.1 The general nature of the tax 130
8.2 The system illustrated 131
8.3 Taxable supplies.. 132
8.4 The tax point.. 132
8.5 Administration.. 133
8.6 Exempt traders 136
8.7 Exempt goods and services 137
8.8 Zero-rated supplies 138
8.9 The lower 5% rate 140
8.10 Miscellaneous.. 141
8.11 Motor cars... 141
8.12 Retailers 144
8.13 Bad debts 144
8.14 Directors' accommodation.......................... 144
8.15 Treatment for income and corporation tax... 145
8.16 Single European market............................. 145

9 Inheritance Tax.. **146**
9.1 General nature of the tax............................. 146
9.2 Exemptions.. 146
9.3 The value transferred 147
9.4 Gifts within seven years prior to death 148
9.5 Tapering relief... 148
9.6 Potentially exempt transfers (PET).............. 148
9.7 Gifts with reservation.................................. 149
9.8 Other reliefs.. 149
9.9 Re-arrangement of estates.......................... 151
9.10 General conclusions.................................. 152

Note to readers **153**

Index **155**

Summary of Rates and Allowances

A. RATES OF TAX

1. Income Tax (Net income after allowances) – non-savings income

2014/15		2013/14	
£0 to £31,865	20%	£0 to £32,010	20%
£31,866-150,000	40%	£32,011-150,000	40%
above £150,000	45%	above £150,000	45%

(see page page 56 for details of the rates of tax payable on savings income)

2. Corporation Tax

	2014/15	2013/14
Small Profits Rate: £0-£300,000	20%	20%
Intermediate Profits: £300,001-£1.5m	21.25%	23.75%
Large Profits Rate: £1.5m +	21%	23%
Standard fraction: £300,000-£1.5m	1/400	3/400

3. Capital Gains Tax

	2014/15	2013/14
(a) Individuals		
Exemption limits:	£11,000	£10,900
Tax rate:		
basic-rate taxpayers	18%	18%
higher-rate taxpayers*	28%	28%

(b) Companies
At the corporation tax rate

(c) Trusts		
Interest in possession trusts	28%	28%
Discretionary and A&M trusts	28%	28%
Exemption limits	£5,500	£5,450

4. Value Added Tax

	from 1.4.14	from 1.4.13
Registration limit	£81,000	£79,000
Deregistration limit	£79,000	£77,000
Tax rate:		
from 1.12.08 to 31.12.09	15%	
from 1.1.10 to 3.1.11	17.5%	
from 4.1.11	20%	

5. Inheritance Tax

	2014/15	2013/14
Zero band limit	£325,000	£325,000
Excess charged at	40%	40%

B. PERSONAL ALLOWANCES

	2014/15 £	2013/14 £
Personal allowance*:		
Standard (born after 5 April 1948)	10,000	9,440
Born between 6 April 1938 and 5 April 1948	10,500	10,500
Born before 6 April 1938	10,660	10,660
Blind person's allowance	2,230	2,160
Married couple's allowance**		
Basic allowance	3,140	3,040
Age 75 or over	8,165	7,915
Income limit for age-related allowances ***	27,000	26,100

* From 2010/11 tax year the Personal Allowance reduces where the income is above £100,000 – by £1 for every £2 of income above the £100,000 limit. This applies irrespective of age.

** Restricted to 10%.

*** If income exceeds this, then the age allowances are reduced by 50% of the excess down to the minimum amount. In the case of personal allowances, down to £10,000 (2013/14 £9,440). In the case of married couple's allowance, down to £3,140 (2013/14 £3,040).

C. TAX CREDITS

Working Tax Credit (WTC)

	2014/15 £	2013/14 £
Annual		
Basic element	1,940	1,920
Second adult or lone parent addition	1,990	1,970
30 hour element	800	790
Disability element	2,935	2,855
Severe disability element	1,255	1,220
Weekly		
Childcare element		
– maximum eligible cost for 1 child	175	175
– maximum eligible cost for 2+ children	300	300
Percent of eligible costs covered	70%	70%

Total claim reduced by 41p for every £1 of annual income over £6,420 (unchanged from 2013/14)

Child Tax Credit (CTC)

Annual	2014/15 £	2013/14 £
Family element*	545	545
Child element (per child)†		
– disabled child	3,100	3,015
– severely disabled child	1,255	1,220
– any other child	2,750	2,720
Income rise disregard	5,000	5,000
Income fall disregard	2,500	2,500

Family element starts to be reduced (at 41p for every £1 of additional income) as soon as all other credits have been withdrawn. Where only CTC available, claim reduced by 41p for every £1 of annual income over £16,010 (£15,910 2013/14).

D. NATIONAL INSURANCE

Class1 (employment)	2014/15 £	2013/14 £
Employee (not contracted out)		
Earnings per week		
Band 1	Up to £153: Nil	Up to £149: Nil
Band 2	£153-805: 12%	£149-797: 12%
Band 3	Over £805: 2%	Over £797: 2%
Employer		
Band 1	Up to £153: Nil	Up to £148: Nil
Band 2	Over £153: 13.8%	Over £148: 13.8%
Class 2 (self-employment)		
Weekly stamp	£2.75	£2.70
No contribution if profits below	£5,885	£5,725
Class 4 (self-employment)		
Band 1	£7,956-41,865: 9%	£7,755-41,450: 9%
Band 2	Over £41,865: 2%	Over £41,450: 2%

1

The Tax System

1.1 WHY WE NEED TO UNDERSTAND THE SYSTEM

As citizens, we should be able to discuss and, if necessary, criticise the government's measures for controlling the economy, in which taxation is an important factor, but we cannot sensibly do so without at least a basic understanding of the system. A more direct reason is that we are all entitled to arrange our affairs so that our personal tax liabilities are reduced to the legal minimum, and this, too, requires knowledge. Of equal importance is that we need to know how to avoid getting into financial difficulties in meeting the tax we are due to pay.

Many people are paying more tax than they need. This is not normally the fault of the tax offices, although mistakes do occur, and in simple cases, the situation can be easily remedied by the individual concerned. In more complicated cases it is desirable to obtain expert advice, but it is necessary to know when to seek that advice.

1.2 WHY TAXES ARE NECESSARY

The purposes for which taxation is required may be summarised as follows.

- Taxation is needed to pay for national expenditure on, for example, defence, government administration and interest on government borrowings – and in years like this one, on extensive military activity abroad; and for local expenditure such as for local services, health, education, welfare and interest on loans. National expenditure is met from taxes such as income tax, corporation tax, capital gains tax, and from customs and excise duties, such as value added tax, stamp duties and licence duties. Local expenditure is met from the rates, the council tax, and from grants from central government.

- Taxation is needed to enforce government financial policy, such as in controlling inflation and encouraging investment in industry.

The tax system is undoubtedly influenced by political motives, both in the wide and narrow sense. While we all naturally resent paying the tax collector part of our hard-earned income, and feel that the burden on us individually is excessive, a principle of taxation is that it should be equitable as between one person and another. Everyone is, of course, entitled to their opinion as to the fairness of the system, but that opinion should be justified by knowledge.

1.3 LIABILITY TO TAX

All individuals resident in the United Kingdom of Great Britain and Northern Ireland are liable to pay income tax, capital gains tax and inheritance tax. Persons resident outside the UK, so far as they derive income from UK sources, are also liable to pay UK tax whether they are British subjects or not. Persons resident in the UK and receiving income from abroad are, in general, liable to UK tax on their overseas earnings, subject to certain reliefs and allowances. Companies are liable for corporation tax on income wherever it arises.

1.4 TAX RETURNS

All persons liable to UK taxation have a duty to make this known to HM Revenue & Customs (HMRC) and to complete Tax Returns if requested and to submit them to the appropriate Inspector of Taxes. The form for a particular tax year shows the income received (including capital gains) and the applicable charges against income, as well as the allowances claimed for the current tax year. Inspectors of Taxes normally send out Self-Assessment Tax Return forms early in each tax year, but they may not do so where all a taxpayer's income is covered by deduction of tax at source such as under the PAYE system for salaries and wages. (See 2.2 Self-Assessment).

There are two separate filing dates. For paper returns the filing deadline is 31 October (for 2013/14 that means a filing deadline of 31 October 2014). For returns filed online the filing deadline is 31 January (for 2013/14 that means a filing deadline of 31 January 2015).

Taxpayers filing paper returns who want HMRC to calculate their tax liability for them will need to file their tax returns by 31 October. The previous cut-off date of 30 September was moved to align with the new paper return filing deadline.

An automatic penalty of £100 is charged to individual taxpayers who fail to file a tax return by the appropriate deadline. For tax years up to 2009/10 the late filing penalty was reduced where a taxpayer's self-assessment tax liability was less than £100. For example, a taxpayer filing a late 2009/10 return showing no liability to tax would pay no late filing penalty. However, from 6 April 2011 taxpayers filing late self-assessment returns will be liable to a penalty of £100 even if their tax liability for the year is less than £100. There are additional penalties where returns are more than 3 months late. Daily penalties of £10 per day are charged (up to maximum of £900) and, if a return is more than 6 months late, there is an additional penalty calculated as the greater of £300 or 5% of the tax liability. This means that if a return is filed more than 6 months late the late filing penalty will be at least £1,300.

It is especially necessary to submit a Return to obtain all available tax allowances; to record investment income from shares, deposits and loans; to record sales and purchases of investments and other assets for capital gains; to record charges on income, such as mortgages and covenants, etc.; and to show where liability to higher rate tax may apply. It is particularly necessary to show untaxed income on the Return: for instance, interest not subject to deduction of tax at source, such as on many national savings and certain government securities. For individuals with small incomes, the submission of a full return may result in a refund of excess tax suffered by deduction from income.

Failure to make a Return, or the submission of a false or incorrect Return, does involve interest and penalties. The Government is in the midst of implementing a new aligned penalty regime which applies to the late filing of returns and late payment of tax. The rules are intended to produce a proportionate response, ranging from the removal of penalties where a time to pay arrangement has been agreed, to significantly higher penalties in the case of prolonged and repeated delay. The new regime applies to Income Tax, Corporation Tax, PAYE, NIC, the construction industry scheme, Stamp Duty Land Tax, Stamp Duty Reserve Tax, Inheritance Tax, pension schemes and Petroleum Revenue Tax.

1.5   SERVICES FROM HM REVENUE AND CUSTOMS

Information and advice on tax is available from numerous Tax Enquiry Centres, including Mobile Centres, but HMRC is not obliged to advise on how tax can be reduced and certainly not on how it can be evaded. A wide range of leaflets is available from the HMRC website (www.hmrc.gov.uk) or from Tax Offices. Complaints may be made to an Adjudicator with regard to the manner in which HMRC has acted, but not on technical matters.

1.6   MINIMISING YOUR TAX

For the purpose of reducing your tax to the minimum legally payable, you should ask yourself the following questions:

- **Are you obtaining all the allowances to which you are entitled?** – See Chapter 2, *Personal Taxation*. If not, you may have failed to make the necessary returns to the Inspector of Taxes.

- **Do you have a balance of income, after deducting allowances and charges, on which tax is payable?** If not, you can reclaim from the Inland Revenue any excess tax deducted from interest, pensions, etc. Many married women, widows, divorcees, retired people and others with low income are liable for little if any tax and could recover some or all of the tax deducted at source from their income.

- **If you are in business, even as a spare time venture, are you charging all allowable expenses in your business accounts?** (See Chapter 4, *Business Taxation*.) Allowable expenses may include, for example, the business use of a car or reasonable fees or salaries paid to spouses or other relatives who assist in the business. Of particular importance are claims for capital allowances and the selection of starting dates.

- **Have you arranged your financial affairs so as to reduce your tax liabilities?** These arrangements could include, for instance, transfers of investments between husband and wife; lifetime gifts to reduce inheritance tax; obtaining exemptions from capital gains tax; taking advantage of personal pensions and various tax-free investments. Reference should be made to the relevant chapters and sections of this book.

In this context, we cannot over-emphasise the dangers of attempting to evade tax by, for example, deliberately omitting to declare income or falsifying the figures. The penalties, both personal and monetary, can be severe, and the tax authorities have many sources of information. (Tax avoidance, on the other hand, by legitimate means, is perfectly acceptable and indeed strongly advisable!) Whilst it is true that some of the more "aggressive" forms of tax avoidance have been severely criticised over the past year or so, it is still the case that, as Lord Tomlin stated in *IRC v Duke of Westminster* (1936):

> *"Every man is entitled if he can to arrange his affairs so that the tax attaching under the appropriate Acts is less than it otherwise would be. If he succeeds in ordering them so as to secure that result, then, however unappreciative the Commissioners of the Inland Revenue or his fellow taxpayers may be of his ingenuity, he cannot be compelled to pay an increased tax" (IRC v Duke of Westminster [1936] AC1 (HL)).*

The difficulty in labelling some forms of tax avoidance as "aggressive" or "morally repugnant" lies in where to draw the line between what is and what is not acceptable tax avoidance.

In a complicated situation, expert advice from a qualified accountant or solicitor specialising in the subject is necessary. The taxpayer should be wary of unqualified advisers or lounge-bar boasting! A great deal of information can be found on the HMRC website (www.hmrc.gov.uk).

In the more straightforward situations, the information contained in the following pages will be sufficient for the taxpayer to manage his or her own tax affairs; it will also show when specialist advice is needed.

1.7 PROVIDING FOR PAYMENT

Most of the income tax due is collected by deduction from income. One example of this is the system for deducting tax from wages and salaries known as the Pay As You Earn system (PAYE). Under this system, the amount of tax deducted is controlled by a code which is notified to the employer. If the code has been correctly allocated, the amount of tax deducted will equal the amount due from the employee during the year. Another example is the deduction of tax at source from investment income such as interest. In this case the tax is deducted at a flat rate regardless of the person's tax liability.

HM Revenue and Customs may require anyone with taxable income not taxed at source, or who it believes may be liable to higher rate tax to complete an annual self-assessment tax return. Almost all company directors and partners are required to complete self-assessment tax returns. If the additional tax payable under self-assessment amounts to more than 20% of the total annual tax liability, the taxpayer will have to make payments on account, as well as any final balancing payment due by 31st January after the end of the tax year. For any tax year, the self-assessment system may result in the taxpayer making three payments of Income Tax and (if applicable) one payment of Capital Gains Tax. The usual pattern of payments will be:

31 January in year of assessment: *first payment on account of Income Tax*

31 July after year of assessment: *second payment on account of Income Tax*

31 January after year of assessment: *final payment to settle the Income Tax liability for the year ... and*

    due payment date for any Capital Gains Tax liability.

Payments on account are not required if the relevant amount is less than £1,000. Also payments on account are not required from taxpayers who paid 80% or more of their tax liability for the previous year through PAYE or other deduction at source. For this purpose, 'relevant amount' means the amount by which Income Tax and Class 4 National Insurance contributions due in the previous tax year exceed the amount of Income Tax deducted at source.

Capital gains tax is payable on 31 January following the tax year in which the gain arose.

Companies are charged to **corporation tax** on all taxable income and gains. The assessment is based on the accounting period, and (in most cases) the tax is payable nine months after the end of that period.

Where tax is not paid on time, the Collector of Taxes will issue demands, and will charge interest on tax paid late.

It is important to avoid financial difficulties when large demands for tax are received. This applies, in particular, to business profits, higher-rate income tax, and tax on untaxed interest. The remedy is to provide for the tax in advance through regular savings out of current income, but for that purpose it is necessary to know when the tax will become due and to be able to forecast the amount.

In some cases, people fail to make returns to the Inspector of Taxes, or make incorrect returns, of the income they receive. This particularly applies to occasional work and spare-time activities. This may be due to ignorance of the tax regulations or genuine mistakes, but the almost inevitable consequence is that tax demands on the undeclared income are received going back for six years, or longer where there is fraud. In the latter case, severe penalties may be charged in addition to the tax due. Delay in payment will give rise to interest being charged in addition.

In 2014, the last date to notify HMRC of chargeability to tax for 2013/14 is 5 October 2014. Failure to do so may lead to a penalty of up to 100% of any tax paid late. The newly self-employed have to notify the Inland Revenue of starting to trade within 3 months of the end of the month in which they started – for example, if you started your business on 1 May 2014 you have until 31 August 2014 to notify. Otherwise, a penalty of £100 is due.

If you are required to complete a self-assessment return, HMRC will send you a self-assessment form at the end of the tax year to be assessed, unless you submitted an electronic tax return for the previous year, in which case HMRC will send you a notice to complete a self-assessment tax return on the assumption that you will be submitting an electronic tax return and will not require a paper return. The self-assessment tax return for 2013/14 was issued in April 2014. In circumstances where payments on account are required (see page 16), a sum of tax, based on the 2012/13 actual liability will already have been paid by 31 January 2014, and a similar sum is due on 31 July 2014. The tax return itself need not be returned to the HMRC until 31 October 2014 in the case of paper returns or 31 January 2015 in the case of returns filed online. On this date, the balance of any tax due must be paid. This date should be kept to in order to avoid penalties and interest.

Collectors will not hesitate to take legal action to obtain long overdue tax. They may sue in the Courts, and distrain on the taxpayer's furniture and effects. Many people have been made bankrupt and companies liquidated for unpaid tax.

Certificates of Tax Deposit may be obtained to provide for the potential liability for income tax which is in dispute, thus avoiding an interest charge.

1.8   THE ADMINISTRATION OF THE SYSTEM

How taxation is authorised

The statutory authority for the imposition of taxation is contained in the following Acts of Parliament.

- *Income and Corporation Taxes Act 1988* (a Consolidating Act)
- The *Taxes Management Act 1970*, covering the administration of taxation
- The *Provisional Collection of Taxes Act 1968*, permitting the Budget proposals to be enforced until amended
- The *Capital Allowances Act 2001*, providing for allowances on the acquisition of fixed assets by business instead of depreciation.
- *Taxation of Chargeable Gains Act 1992*
- *Value Added Tax Act 1994*
- *Inheritance Tax Act 1984*
- *Income Tax (Earnings and Pensions) Act 2003*
- *Income Tax (Trading and Other Income) Act 2005*
- *Income Tax Act 2007*

This legislation is amended by the annual (usually July) and sometimes more frequent Finance Acts.

This enormous volume of legislation has to be interpreted by the Courts in an even greater volume of decided cases. In addition, the Inland Revenue from time to time publish 'concessions and practice notes', where the strict application of the law would be unjust or unworkable, and to indicate the methods they employ in particular situations.

Proposed amendments and additions to the current law and practice of taxation are presented to Parliament by the Chancellor of the Exchequer by way of a pre-Budget speech in December, and in his Budget Speech, usually in March of each year. Occasionally, especially in an election year, there may be more than one Budget. The 'Budget' is essentially a forecast of government income and expenditure for the coming year, and includes a review of the previous year's results.

The Budget proposals are set out in the Finance Bill which is then debated in Parliament. The provisions of the Finance Bill have immediate effect under the *Provisional Collection of Taxes Act*. Amendments made during the debate are incorporated in the *Finance Act* of the following July which may entail adjustments to the taxation provisionally imposed.

Some historical notes

The fifty-plus years since World War II have seen greater social and economic changes than any other comparable period. The National Health Service was introduced in 1948, and the phrases 'Welfare State' and 'cradle to grave' began to be used to reflect a wide range of social provisions including broader national insurance provisions, the introduction of child allowances, the raising of the school-leaving age and increased old age pensions. Many of these provisions were based on the Beveridge Report of 1942.

Reflecting changes in society, income tax provisions have changed too.

To avoid double taxation arising by tax being charged in two countries on the same income, special arrangements have been in place within the British Empire from 1916. The first agreement with a non-Empire country was with the United States in 1945. Britain now has more agreements with other countries than any other nation.

Corporation Tax on company profits and Capital Gains Tax on long-term gains were introduced by Chancellor James Callaghan in 1965. Callaghan – later Prime Minister and Lord Callaghan (1912-2005) – had previously been an Inland Revenue employee and trade unionist.

Value Added Tax – replacing purchase tax – was introduced in 1973 to be collected by Customs and Excise. William Pitt may have applauded it over income tax because the individual can regulate how much is paid. He or she can simply not buy that item or so many of them – and food, children's clothes and books and newspapers are zero-rated.

Surtax – introduced as super-tax by Lloyd George in 1909 and attacked in Beatle George Harrison's 'Taxman' (Let me tell you how it will be, there's one for you, nineteen for me, 'cause I'm the taxman) – was removed in 1973, but replaced by higher rates of income tax for those with high incomes.

Since 1990, a married woman has been taxed independently on her own income with her own personal allowance. The fight for equality in tax had begun with the *Married Women's Property Act* of 1882.

Special rates have been introduced twice within the post-war years, causing income tax in certain circumstances to exceed 100%.

- For 1947-48, a special contribution was payable when a person's total income exceeded £2,000. For investment income over £5,000 it was 50%. So with income tax at 45% and surtax at 52.5%, the effective rate was 147.5%.
- In 1967-68, the special charge was imposed. For investment income over £8,000, the rate was 45% which – with income tax at 41.25% and surtax at 50% – meant a total rate of 136.25%.

The fiscal year and the assessment year

The government accounting year for taxation purposes, or the 'fiscal year', ends on 5 April, and income tax assessments are made for each year ending on that date. There is a slight difference in the assessment year for corporation tax on limited companies and other corporate bodies and in these cases the 'financial year' ends on 31 March, thus conforming to the standard 'reference year' for such bodies under the Companies Acts.

For most of an individual's income – for example, income from employment – tax is calculated on the actual amount received in the year of assessment, at the rates of tax applicable to that year. For some income, notably the profits of a partnership or business in single ownership, the assessment year will normally cover the income shown by the accounts made up to a date in the year of assessment.

Corporate bodies, including limited companies, are charged to corporation tax on the taxable profits shown by their accounts for their accounting years. The rate of corporation tax applied is the rate applicable to the tax years covered by the accounting period. This is payable 9 months after the year end.

The structure of HM Revenue and Customs

HM Revenue & Customs (HMRC) was formed on the 18 April 2005, following the merger of Inland Revenue and HM Customs and Excise Departments

HM Revenue and Customs brings together the direct taxes and other duties that were previously administered by the Inland Revenue and the indirect taxes and customs functions that were dealt with by HM Customs and Excise (HMCE).

Although the two bodies are now one department, the actual integration of the two is expected to take several years. A major review of HMRC's powers is underway with a view to rationalising the previously separate powers of the Inland Revenue and HM Customs and Excise. Large parts of the *Finance Act 2008* were devoted to the results of this ongoing review including sections devoted to HMRC information powers, record keeping and penalties for errors.

The Commissioners of HMRC answer to the Treasury and ultimately to the Chancellor of the Exchequer. The structure below the Commissioners is complex. Previously the country was divided into tax districts headed by an inspector of taxes who assessed taxpayers' tax liabilities. Tax was collected by collectors of taxes. Following the merger of the Inland Revenue and HM Customs and Excise all staff exercising the roles of inspectors or collectors are full time civil servants appointed by HM Revenue and Customs. They are known as Officers of HM Revenue and Customs.

The tax assessment and collection functions have been brought together in Taxpayer Service Offices (TSOs). These offices deal with the more routine work in respect of assessment and collection. For each district, there is a Taxpayers District Office, which deals with local companies and with technical and compliance issues.

As from 1 April 2009 the whole system of tax appeals was radically changed. As from that date the general commissioners, special commissioners and VAT Tribunals ceased to exist and were replaced by first tier and second tier tribunals. Essentially, the first tier tribunal will hear all tax appeals and the chief function of the second tier tribunal will be to hear appeals from the first tier tribunal.

Money laundering

Any new clients who approach any firm, be they accountants, lawyers, banks, estate agents or whatever, have to provide personal details such as passport, driving licence and current utilities bill, in order to prove that they are who they say they are. Photocopies of these documents must be filed as evidence that checks have been made. Failure to do so will render the adviser firm liable to prosecution. Similar threats of possible liability for advisers now exist if that adviser suspects or has knowledge of fraud, and it is not reported to NCA (National Crimes Agency).

Advisers are also obliged to report to NCA in the case of clients who refuse to correct errors which result in a loss of tax to the Exchequer.

1.9 THE CATEGORIES OF TAX

Everyone pays tax in one form or another. We all suffer value added tax (VAT) on many purchases; most of us pay income tax, the council tax and National Insurance contributions; many are liable for capital gains tax. Companies pay corporation tax, capital gains tax, excise duties, VAT and business rates. For a full understanding of the system it is therefore desirable to consider all the taxes in which we may be involved.

Taxes are usually described as either direct or indirect and this classification is used below, although the distinction between the two categories is not always precise. Direct taxes are those charged directly on individuals, partnerships, trusts and corporate bodies and indirect taxes are of more general application and collected by an intermediary.

(a) Direct taxes

Income tax. This is charged on the total income of individuals, including their salaries, wages, pensions, fees and other remuneration; their dividends, interest and royalties; profits from businesses they operate alone or in partnership; and many other kinds of income, including for example, certain National Insurance benefits, alimony, etc. The rate of tax payable depends on the type of income. A distinction must be made between non-savings income, dividends and other savings income.

For non-savings income, the income tax rates on taxable income are as follows:

	2014/15		2013/14	
	Band £	Rate %	Band £	Rate %
Basic	0-£31,865	20%	0-£32,010	20%
Higher	£31,866-£150,000	40%	£32,011-£150,000	40%
Additional	over £150,000	45%	over £150,000	45%

In the case of most savings income other than dividends, tax is deducted at source at the lower rate of 20%. Taxpayers with taxable income below the basic rate upper limit have no further tax to pay. Those with income above the higher or additional rate limits have to pay a further 20 or 30%.

UK dividends are paid net of a tax credit of 10% of the gross dividend. Basic rate taxpayers have no further tax to pay, but higher rate taxpayers have a further liability of 22.5% and additional rate taxpayers a further 27.5%.

In the case of savings income other than dividends, there is a starting rate of 10%, applicable on savings income up to £2,880 (2013/14 £2,790), provided that total *non*-savings income does not exceed the personal allowance plus £2,790. For further details see page 56. In 2015/16, the starting rate will be reduced to 0% and the savings band will increase to £5,000.

Corporation tax. This is payable by limited companies and other corporate bodies on their profits, at 20% (21% in the year ended 31 March 2014) for large companies and 20% for small companies. Profits charged to corporation tax include both income and capital gains.

Capital gains tax. For 2008/09 and 2009/10, capital gains tax at a flat rate of 18% was chargeable on gains by individuals above the annual exemption limit. For 2010/11 gains realised before 23 June 2010 were taxed at a flat rate of 18% irrespective of an individual's income. For gains realised on or after 23 June 2010 the rate of capital gains tax is calculated by reference to an individual's income. Gains that fall within an individual's unused basic rate income tax band are taxed at 18%. To the extent that the total of chargeable gains exceeds an individual's unused basic rate income tax basic rate band they are taxed at 28%. For 2014/15 the first £11,000 of an individual's capital gains are exempt from tax (2013/14 £10,900).

Inheritance tax. This is payable on certain lifetime transfers and by the personal representatives of deceased persons on wealth passing on death.

For the tax years 6 April 2009 to 5 April 2018 the tax begins when total capital passing on death or lifetime transfers exceeds £325,000. Certain lifetime transfers ('chargeable lifetime transfers') are subject to an immediate tax charge at 20%, with a further potential charge of up to 20% payable on death. The rate of tax on transfers after death is 40%. There are many exemptions.

Rates and the Council Tax. This is a uniform business rate is payable by businesses on the assessed letting value of land and buildings, and the council tax is payable on domestic accommodation.

National Insurance contributions. These are effectively a tax although not normally so regarded by the Government.

(b) Indirect taxes

Customs and Excise duties. These are chargeable on certain dutiable goods imported and those produced in the UK, such as liquors and tobacco. This category also includes various licence fees and stamp duties.

Value added tax (VAT). This is administered by the Customs and Excise and chargeable on the sales value of goods and services, with many exemptions and zero-rated items. It is payable through the whole chain of importers, producers and distributors, less tax on purchases, but ultimately borne by the consumer. It is chargeable at the rate of 20% from 1 January 2011 (17.5% for the year ended 31 December 2010).

1.10 THE SCHEDULAR SYSTEM OF DIRECT TAXATION

The schedular system of direct taxation was originally introduced in 1803. The *Income Tax (Trading and Other Income) Act 2005* (ITTOIA 2005) which entered into force on 6 April 2005 has abolished this system in so far as it applies to Income Tax – it did remain for Corporation Tax until 26 March 2009 when the *Corporation Tax Act 2009* received royal assent.

Schedules A, D, E and F are now referred to respectively as property income, trading income, employment income and investment income in the hope that such terms are likely to be more meaningful to the layman.

Foreign sources of income are now included with their equivalent UK source rather than being classified separately, but with the special rules relating to foreign income being contained in a separate part of the Act.

2

Personal Taxation

2.1 ASSESSING THE LIABILITY

An individual is liable for income tax on the whole of his or her income which is chargeable to tax. That income may include, for example, remuneration from employment, business profit, rents from letting property or rooms, and income from investments. Very little income escapes the tax net. There may also be a liability for capital gains tax which is considered in Chapter 5.

From the gross income of a taxpayer from all sources, certain charges on income are deductible, such as eligible interest and royalties. Gifts and living expenses are not allowable deductions. Personal reliefs and allowances are then deducted from the remaining amount, called 'total income', to produce a balance on which income tax is charged, the 'taxable' income.

In 2014/15, income tax will be charged as described previously on page 22, but shown again here:

	2014/15		2013/14	
	Band £	Rate %	Band £	Rate %
Basic	0-£31,865	20%	0-£32,010	20%
Higher	£31,866-£150,000	40%	£32,011-£150,000	40%
Additional	over £150,000	45%	over £150,000	45%

For the purpose of calculating the higher rate payable, interest received net of tax and dividends must be 'grossed up'. Grossing up means calculating the amount of the interest or dividend by adding back tax which has been deducted.

The tax payable by an employed taxpayer or pensioner will normally be accounted for by PAYE deductions from the pay or occupational pension.

However, the actual tax liability will often need re-calculation after the end of the tax year leaving an amount underpaid or overpaid. The adjustments may be due, for instance, to incorrect codings for PAYE, and the correction of estimates, e.g. state pensions, income from property and investment income, not taxed at source.

Business profits made by the self-employed or partners are included, with all other sources and income, on the self-assessment tax return (see 2.2 below).

2.2 SELF-ASSESSMENT

Readers who require specific guidance on how to complete their Self-Assessment Tax Return, should refer to the comprehensive Guide which accompanies the tax return. This will take them through the maze and lead, in most cases, to a successful and accurate completion of the return for which they are legally responsible. In more complex cases readers are advised to seek professional help in completing their self-assessment tax returns.

The Government is actively encouraging taxpayers to file their self-assessment tax returns online. There are also several organisations which offer online services for assessment, advice about tax coding and general tax saving. If you wish to follow this route, then an initial approach with a search engine such as Ask.com will bring up quite a list of relevant sites (and some oddities). For information about self-assessment online, go direct to **www.hmrc.gov.uk**. Some of the advantages of doing your self-assessment online are:

- automatic calculation of your tax as you complete the return
- internet returns are processed faster
- any money owed you by the IR is paid faster
- online acknowledgement of your return is given on receipt
- it is safe, secure and more convenient – the service can be used day or night
- the web pages provide comprehensive information and assistance in all aspects of self-assessment.

2.3 MINIMISING THE LIABILITY

Careful study of this chapter will indicate how in many cases an individual's tax liability can be reduced. This subject was discussed in Chapter 1, section 1.6, but is worth repetition. In particular consideration should be given to the following courses of action:

☑ Obtain all the possible reliefs and allowances.

☑ Take advantage of opportunities for tax-free investments, as discussed in Chapter 3, *Investment Income*.

☑ A married couple should ensure that no allowances are lost because one partner has insufficient taxable income. This could be achieved by, for example, transferring investments to the party with insufficient income, or ensuring that an adequate but defendable salary is paid to that party for services to a business carried out by the other partner. The transfer of investments may also be effective in reducing inheritance tax.

☑ One party's liability for higher rate tax may be reduced or eliminated by a transfer of income to the other party in the manner suggested above.

☑ Where income is received from self-employment, part-time work or an unincorporated business owned by the taxpayer, ensure that all allowable expenses are charged in the business accounts.

☑ Where one spouse's potential capital gains are likely to exceed the annual threshold of £10,900 in 2013/14 (£10,600 in 2012/13), it could be beneficial to consider transferring some of those investments to the other spouse before realising the gains to make use of the other spouse's annual exemption.

2.4   SPECIMEN COMPUTATIONS

(a) Basic rate taxpayer

J Smith is a single man aged 30 with the following sources of income in 2014/15:

	£
Income from employment	30,000
(PAYE deducted at source £4,000)	
Income from rented properties	3,650
Dividends (net)	900
Bank interest (net)	1,600

Mr Smith's tax liability for 2014/15 can be arrived at as follows:

	Non-savings income £	Savings income £	Dividend income £	Tax deducted at source £
Employment earnings	30,000			4,000
Property income	3,650			
Dividends (10/9)			1,000	100
Taxed interest – bank interest (100/80)		2,000		400
Statutory total income	33,650	2,000	1,000	4,500
Single person's allowance	(10,000)			
Taxable income	23,650	2,000	1,000	

Tax:	£
£23,650 @ 20%	4,730.00
£2,000 @ 20%	400.00
£1,000 @ 10%	100.00
Tax borne	5,230.00
Less:	
Tax deducted at source and tax credit on dividend	(4,500.00)
Tax due	730.00

(b) Higher Rate Taxpayer

If Mr Smith's income from employment for the year had been £41,000 with PAYE deducted of £6,200, his tax liability would be arrived at as follows:

	Non-savings income £	Savings income £	Dividend income £	Tax deducted at source £
Employment earnings	41,000			6,200
Property income	3,650			
Dividends (10/9)			1,000	100
Taxed interest – bank interest (100/80)		2,000		400
Statutory total income	44,650	2,000	1,000	6,700
Single person's allowance	(10,000)			
Taxable income	34,650	2,000	1,000	

Tax:	£
£31,865 @ 20%	6,373.00
£2,785 @ 40%	1,114.00
£2,000 @ 40%	800.00
£1,000 @ 32.5%	325.00
Tax borne	8,612.00
Less:	
Tax deducted at source and tax credit on dividend	(6,700.00)
Tax due	1,912.00

2.5   RELIEFS AND ALLOWANCES

(a) Personal allowance

This allowance is available to persons of either sex (including children), whether married or not. Thus, under independent taxation, both husband and wife obtain the allowance. The allowance depends on the age of the taxpayer. In 2013/14 the basis for assessing eligibility was changed to refer to date of birth rather than age. The allowances for 2013/14 and 2014/15 are set out below:

	2014/15 £	2013/14 £
Born after 5 April 1948	10,000	9,440
Born between 6 April 1938 and 5 April 1948	10,500	10,500
Born before 6 April 1938	10,660	10,660

The personal allowance reduces where the income is above £100,000 – by £1 for every £2 of income above the £100,000 limit. This applies irrespective of age.

From 2013/14 the age-related personal allowances will not be increased. People born on or after 6 April 1948 will only be entitled to a standard personal allowance.

The income limit for age-related allowances is £27,000 in 2014/15 (£26,100 in 2013/4). If income exceeds this, then the age-related allowances are reduced by 50% of the excess down to the minimum amount – in the case of personal allowances, down to the under-65 amount.

(b) Married couple's allowance, widow's bereavement allowance, and child allowance

From 6 April 2000, these allowances were mostly abolished. Only a small part of one allowance remains. The married couple's allowance is only available to couples where one of the partners was born before 6 April 1935 (i.e. over 79 at the end of the tax year 2014/15).

Married couple's allowance. For couples married on or before 5 December 2005, this allowance is given to the husband; for couples married after 5 December 2005, the allowance is given to the partner earning the higher income of the two. The tax relief on the allowance is restricted in to 10%.

The allowance is as follows:

	2014/15 £	2013/14 £
Married couple's allowance	8,165	7,915

The allowance is reduced by half of the amount by which the taxpayer's income exceeds £27,000 in 2014/15 (£26,100 in 2013/14). The minimum allowance for 2014/15 is £3,140 (2013/14 £3,040).

For more information, visit www.hmrc.gov.uk/incometax/married-allow.htm. Widow's bereavement allowance and child allowance have been abolished.

(c) Blind persons

If the taxpayer is registered as a blind person for the whole or part of a year, an allowance of £2,230 in 2014/15 (2013/14 £2,160) may be claimed. Where the allowance is not needed, it can in certain circumstances be transferred to the taxpayer's husband or wife. By concession, the allowance is available for the year previous to the year of registration on proof of blindness at the end of that previous year.

2.6 CHILDREN

Child benefits. These are cash payments payable to mothers in respect of children under 19 years of age (*Child Benefit Act 1975*). The payments are exempt from tax.

Where child benefits do not apply. Child benefits may not be payable in respect of children under 19 years of age living in certain overseas countries – for example, the former USSR, Asia, India, Pakistan, Africa and the Americas – where there are no reciprocal arrangements for social security benefits.

Scholarships. Income from a scholarship for full-time education is exempt from income tax so far as the holder of the scholarship is concerned. However, in the case of a scholarship paid for by the employer of a director or employee earning £8,500 p.a. or more, the cash value of a scholarship for a member of their family will normally be treated as part of their remuneration, subject to qualifications where payment is made from a trust fund.

Adopted children. By an extra-statutory concession in 1983, no tax will be charged on allowances paid to people who adopt children under government-approved schemes.

Child care. No tax is payable by an employee for the value of a place in a nursery provided by the employer for the employee's child. Tax is however payable by an employee on a cash allowance, voucher for child care or fees paid for child care if paid by the employer to the employee. Fees paid by the employer direct to nurseries, etc., and minders are taxable on directors and on employees earning £8,500 or more.

Tax credits

The Child Tax Credit and the Working Tax Credit were introduced from April

2003 to support families with children, tackle poverty and make work pay.

The **Child Tax Credit** brings together the various strands of support for families with children – the child elements in Income Support, Jobseeker's Allowance, Working Families' Tax Credit (WFTC), Disabled Person's Tax Credit (DPTC) and the Children's Tax Credit – into one streamlined system.

The **Working Tax Credit** broadly replicates the adult support in WFTC and extends the principles of WFTC and DPTC to adults without children to create one transparent instrument to make work pay, paid through the wage packet. It also includes support with the costs of childcare, building on the success of the existing childcare component of WFTC and DPTC.

Universal credit

Draft legislation has been published for the replacement system of universal credit which is due to be phased in between October 2013 and the end of 2017. Universal credit will cover the same recipients as tax credits replacing child and working tax credit, but it will also replace jobseeker's allowance, housing benefit, income support, and income-related employment and support allowance. As with tax credits the universal credit award is based on a system of allowances for individual and family circumstances, less actual income. The process for calculating universal credit is, however, more convoluted than the one for tax credits.

Universal credit will be calculated monthly as opposed to the tax credits' annual period. Self-employed claimants will have to report their net income for the month online every month using a cash basis of accounting.

In the period to 2017 the existing tax credit system will run alongside the universal credit system as existing tax credit claimants are gradually moved across to the universal credit system.

The Child Tax Credit

Child Tax Credit is a payment to support families with children. Claims can be made by an individual, a couple or a polygamous family unit. There are no requirements to be working in order to make a claim.

A claim for Child Tax Credit must be made on form TC600. The same form is also used for claims for Working Tax Credit. Claim forms can be obtained from local Inland Revenue offices, or a form can be completed over the internet (**www.hmrc.gov.uk/taxcredits**).

Child Tax Credit is paid for a child until 1 September following his or her 16th birthday, or for a young person aged 16 to 18 who is in full-time education, up to and including A-levels, NVQ level 3 or Scottish Highers, or a young person aged 16 to 18 who has left full-time education but does not have a job or training place and who has registered with the Careers Service.

Child Tax Credit is paid in addition to Child Benefit and any Working Tax Credit.

The amount of Child Tax Credit to which an individual, couple or family unit is entitled will be calculated by reference to the family income for the year of the claim, the number of children and the hours worked. Claims for 2014/15 will be based initially on income figures for the year ended 5 April 2014, revised to 2014/15 figures once the figures are finalised. Persons claiming Child Tax Credit (or, for that matter, Working Tax Credit) will be required to complete a return at the end of each claim year, giving details of their actual income for that year. This information will be used to revise claims where necessary.

The award can be based either on the previous year's income (PYI) or the current year's income (CYI).

(a) If CYI is greater than PYI by no more than a certain amount (known as an "income disregard"), the final award is based on PYI;

(b) If CYI is greater than PYI by more than the specified income disregard, the final award is based on CYI less the income disregard.

Where the current year's income is LESS than the previous years income (i.e. has fallen):

(a) If PYI exceeds CYI by no more than a certain amount (known as an income disregard) the final award is based on PYI ;

(b) If PYI exceeds CYI by more than the specified income disregard.

The income disregard amount for 2014/15 and 2013/14 is £5,000 for a rise in income and £2,500 for a fall in income, as indicated in the table on page 33.

The entitlements set out in the table are the maximum amounts available. Couples with a combined income of more than £16,010 will get a reduced benefit. For further information on the calculation of entitlement, visit www. hmrc.gov.uk/taxcredits/payments-entitlement/entitlement.

Child Tax Credit (CTC)

Maximum rates (annual)*	2014/15 £	2013/14 £
Family element	545	545
Child element (per child)		
– disabled child	3,100	3,015
– severely disabled child	1,255	1,220
– any other child	2,750	2,720

*Family element starts to be reduced (at 41p for every £1 of additional income) as soon as all other credits have been withdrawn. Where only CTC available, claim reduced by 41p for every £1 of annual income over £16,010 (£15,910 2013/14).

Income rise disregard	5,000	5,000
Income fall disregard	2,500	2,500

The Working Tax Credit

Working Tax Credit is designed to top up the earnings of working people on low incomes, whether or not they have children. It is available to employed or self-employed people and includes support for the costs of qualifying child care.

People who are responsible for a child or a young person can claim Working Tax Credit if they are over 16 and working at least 16 hours per week.

Working Tax Credit (WTC)

Annual	2014/15 £	2013/14 £
Basic element	1,940	1,920
Second adult or lone parent addition	1,990	1,970
30-hour element	800	790
Disability element	2,935	2,855
Severe disability element	1,255	1,220
Weekly		
Childcare element		
– maximum eligible cost for 1 child	175	175
– maximum eligible cost for 2 or more children	300	300
– % of eligible costs covered	70%	70%

Total claim reduced by 41p for every £1 of annual income over £6,420 (unchanged from 2013/14)

People without children can claim WTC provided:

- they are aged 25 or over and working at least 30 hours per week
- they are aged 16 or over and working at least 16 hours per week AND they have a disability which makes getting a job more difficult for them.

Working Tax Credit is paid in addition to Child Tax Credit. The amount depends on the circumstances of the individual or couple.

Some general points to bear in mind with regard to the claiming of Tax Credits

- Tax Credits can only be backdated for a maximum of 1 month. This can create difficulties for people unsure as to whether they will qualify for Tax Credits in 2014/15. HM Revenue and Customs will accept protective claims for Tax Credits from persons uncertain as to what their circumstances for 2014/15 will entitle them.

- Tax Credits are worked out ultimately on the basis of annual average income NOT on an actual basis.

   Example: Mr B is single and is employed from 6 April 2013 to 6 October 2013 at a salary of £30,000 pa. He is made redundant with effect from 6 October 2013 and returns to work on 6 January 2014 on a salary of £24,000.

   For the purposes of calculating any entitlement to Tax Credits, Mr B's annual average income would be:

   $$£30,000 \times 6/12 = \quad £15,000$$
   $$£24,000 \times 3/12 = \quad \underline{£6,000}$$
   $$£21,000$$

- The rules on Tax Credits require notifying HM Revenue and Customs of changes in circumstances within 1 month of the date of change. There are penalties (maximum £300) for failing to notify. Changes in circumstances that require notification to HM Revenue and Customs include:

   (i)   changes in the composition of the credit-claiming unit such as ceasing to be, or becoming, a member of a couple
   (ii) changes in the amount spent on childcare which give rise to a fall in average childcare costs of £10 a week or more, and which last for at least four weeks in a row.

- Changes in income do not have to be notified to HM Revenue and Customs within one month of the date of change, but people may wish to notify such changes to HM Revenue and Customs with a view to getting their claims revised as soon as possible.

- People who make a claim for Tax Credits should be aware that there is no provision for a Tax Credit claim once made, to be withdrawn. This means that, even if they do not qualify for Tax Credits, they must still keep the Inland Revenue informed of changes of circumstances, e.g. the birth of a child or commencement of childcare costs. They will also need to complete the end-of-year return providing details of the Tax Credit-claiming unit's joint income for the year. Thus there could be instances of significant compliance costs without any benefit in terms of being eligible to receive Tax Credits.

- At the end of the tax year, claimants will be sent a renewal form. This form asks for details of income for the year just ended and enables claimants to make a claim for the forthcoming year. For claimants who are only entitled to the family element of child tax credit, the award will automatically be renewed and they only need to respond to the renewal notice if their circumstances have changed. Other claimants must confirm the information in the notice by 31 July following the end of the tax year. Failure to do so could result in the payment of tax credits being stopped.

Child Trust Fund

The Government introduced Child Trust Funds for all children born between 1 September 2002 and 2 January 2011 through which it provided an initial endowment of £250 (£500 for low income families). The 2006 Budget contained an announcement that eligible children would receive a further £250 (or £500) at the age of seven. The fund has other features, including:

- allowing additional contributions to be made by others such as parents, family and friends, of up to £1,200 per year
- accessible at age 18 without restriction
- delivered through open market competition.

All age seven payments have stopped and will not be paid for children who reach age seven after 31 July 2010.

2.7 HUSBAND AND WIFE

In most circumstances the following particular rules apply:

- Each party obtains a personal allowance – £10,000 in 2014/15 (£9,440 in 2013/14). From 2013/14 the age-related personal allowances will not be increased and their availability will be restricted to people born on or before 5 April 1948 for an allowance worth £10,500 and 5 April 1938 for an allowance worth £10,660. From 2015/16 married couples and civil partners who do not pay tax at the higher or additional rates will be able to transfer up to 10% of their personal allowance to their spouse or civil partner.

- Income from property owned jointly by husband and wife is normally assumed to be shared equally. However, from 6 April 2004, income distributions from shares in a close company that are jointly owned by a married couple will no longer automatically be split 50:50, subject to an election for the split to be based on the actual proportion of ownership and entitlement to this income. Instead, distributions (usually dividends) will be taxed according to the actual proportions of ownership and entitlement to the income.

- If one party to a marriage was born before 6 April 1935 and the marriage took place prior to 5 December 2005, a married couple's allowance is claimable. The parties must be living together (or the husband be maintaining a separated wife) for this further allowance to apply. In the year of marriage, it is reduced by 1/12th for each month (beginning on the sixth of each month) before marriage.

- The whole or part of the allowance can be transferred to the wife.

- No transfer of excess allowances is available where the couple are separated, but where the husband is continuing to support the wife he will obtain the further allowance as above. This also applies in reverse.

Civil Partnerships

The *Civil Partnership Act 2004* came into force on 5 December 2005. From that date, the rules described above, regarding husband and wife, apply equally to civil partners.

2.8 SALARIES, WAGES AND DIRECTORS' FEED

Introduction

For most people the greater part, if not the whole, of their income consists of the salary, wages, commission, bonuses and fees they draw under a contract of employment. This part of a taxpayer's income is assessed in accordance with the rules of the charge to tax on employment income. The most important of these rules are considered in this section.

The majority of tax on earnings from employment is collected by deduction under the Pay As You Earn (PAYE) system, which is considered later. Earnings are assessed as income for the year in which they are received (see below).

There are different rules according to (a) whether the taxpayer is resident, ordinarily resident and domiciled in the UK and (b) where the duties of employment are carried out.

The Pay As You Earn system (PAYE)

(a) General. The following notes are intended to indicate only the general nature and scope of the PAYE system. More detailed information is available from Tax Offices where a comprehensive pamphlet, the Employer's Guide to PAYE, can be obtained, or online at www.hmrc.gov.uk/employers.

PAYE is the system under which employers are obliged to deduct income tax and National Insurance contributions from their employees' remuneration. The amount to be deducted is found from tax tables which take into account, by a coding system, the reliefs and allowances to which each employee is entitled. The employee's code is notified by the tax office to the employer and to the employee who, in addition, receives details showing how this particular code is made up. The employee should ensure that he or she is receiving all the applicable reliefs and allowances.

The remuneration from which the deductions are made includes all income from the employment, including salaries, wages, holiday pay, bonuses, fees, commission, pensions (to retired employees), most sickness benefits and some taxable benefits provided by the employer, the amount of which must be notified to the employee.

In order to assist self-assessment employers have to issue their employees a P60 by 31 May of each year.

(b) Benefits. In the case of most benefits provided by the employer, such as the provision of a company car, the benefit will be outside the PAYE deduction scheme. In those cases the benefit will be taken into account in the code, so that the tax collected under PAYE will be increased by the necessary amount. Employers have to provide a copy of Form P11D to the employee by 6 July of each year.

(c) Deductions from pay. Where the remuneration is subject to deduction of the tax under PAYE, the amount to be taken into account is the amount before deductions, such as National Insurance Contributions (NIC) and allowable trade union subscriptions. However, where contributions to the employer's approved pension scheme are allowable, the amount of the contribution will reduce the amount of the pay on which PAYE is operated. Further payments subject to PAYE are redundancy pay where this is taxable, and certain advance payments of directors' fees.

An employee can arrange for contributions to approved charities to be deducted from remuneration and paid by the employer to specific charities, these contributions reducing pay for tax purposes.

(d) Refunds. When an employee has experienced a period of low remuneration, such as during sickness or unemployment, refunds may be due, but no refund can be made while an employee is involved in a trade dispute.

(e) Records. In addition to making correct deductions from employees' pay, an employer has to keep accurate records which may be inspected by tax officials, and submit annual returns; these returns include P11D forms showing the expenses and benefits of directors and employees receiving more than £8,500 p.a., and P9D forms showing expenses of other employees. An employer also has to provide employees with certificates of pay and tax deducted at the end of each tax year, and P45 forms with similar information when an employee leaves the employment.

(f) The codes. Apart from the issue of codes a tax office will not provide an employer with any information about an employee's affairs. The codes do, however, provide some information. Thus a code with the suffix H indicates that the taxpayer receives the married couple's allowance or the additional personal allowance; L indicates the personal allowance; codes P and V include the age allowance for single and married couples respectively. Where an employee does not wish this information disclosed he should apply for code T, which is used for special cases, such as where there is no 'free pay' (i.e. no allowances are given by the code OT) or, where no tax is deductible, code NT. The code BR indicates that the tax is deducted at the basic rate. The prefix D shows that higher rates are payable.

(g) Code K. This applies where coding reductions exceed allowances. The coding reductions might cover occupational pensions, taxable benefits and untaxed income (e.g. on certain savings). Under the old code F the income in excess of the allowances was estimated and could only have the effect of reducing the allowances to nil. As a result the excess of the income over the allowances was subject to assessment at the end of the year. Under the K code such assessments should no longer be necessary as this new code deducts actual income (not estimated income) from the allowances, and if a surplus of income results that amount is added to pay or occupational pension.

Receipts basis of taxing remuneration

(a) General. From 6 April 1989 employees, including directors, have been taxed for a tax year on the remuneration actually received, or assumed to be received in that year. The new basis did not change the system for taxing regular payments of salaries and wages which were already taxed on a receipts basis and were subject to deductions for PAYE. It did, however, affect remuneration which is paid in a tax year after the year in which it is earned. This is often the case where directors' fees and bonuses are dependent on profits and cannot therefore be determined or paid until after the end of the accounting year of the business.

(b) Time of receipt of remuneration. It will be assumed that an individual has received remuneration at the earliest of the following times:

- When payment is made.
- When the employee or director becomes entitled to payment (which may be after the accounting year in which the remuneration is earned). In the case of directors:
    - (i) when remuneration is credited to an employee's or director's account with the paying company – this often happens in smaller companies, where it is the practice to credit remuneration or fees of directors to their current account, and to pay part or all of the balance on that account when the cash position permits
    - (ii) where remuneration is determined during the course of an accounting year, it is assumed to be received at the end of that year
    - (iii) where remuneration for an accounting period is determined after the end of that period, it will be taxed in the fiscal year when it is determined.
- Chargeable benefits are to be treated as received for tax purposes when the benefits are provided.

These rules apply to PAYE deductions.

(c) Treatment in business computation. Remuneration charged in the business accounts in a particular accounting year is, of course, normally an allowable deduction in computing profits for that year. However, if remuneration is paid nine months or more after the end of an accounting period in which it is charged, that remuneration is not deductible in computing that year's taxable profit. It will be observed that where this rule applies the taxable profit for the year when the remuneration arises will be so much greater than the accounts profit.

If a tax calculation is made within the nine-month period, and the remuneration has not then been paid, that remuneration will be disallowed in the calculation, and allowed later when the remuneration is paid. However, the calculation can be adjusted if the remuneration is subsequently paid within the nine-month period; but a claim for this purpose must be made to the Inspector of Taxes within two years of the end of the accounts period concerned.

Compensation for loss of employment

If the compensation arises out of the contract of employment it is taxable in the hands of the recipient, unless paid for disability or injury, special contributions to approved retirement schemes, foreign service (with conditions) and terminal grants to members of the armed forces. By a statutory concession dated 2

September 1993 legal costs received as a result of pursuing a claim are not taxable. Voluntary payments made to an employee after his employment has ceased are exempt from tax up to £30,000. Statutory redundancy pay is also exempt, but does use up part or all of the £30,000 exempt amount.

2.9   TAXABLE BENEFITS

General

Liability to tax may arise on benefits provided for an employee in addition to his salary, and these benefits may be in kind rather than cash. Particular examples of taxable benefits include the use of company cars, free accommodation, loans at beneficial rates, the provision of suits and television sets and free travel and credit card payments.

The general principle is that the cash equivalent of the benefits will be assessed on directors, and on employees earning £8,500 or more (including the value of the benefits). The rules do not apply to full-time working directors earning less than £8,500 who, with their relatives and associates (e.g. partners), own no more than 5% of the company's share capital. Employees earning less than £8,500 may be assessed on benefits received if such benefits are convertible into cash. The cash equivalent will in most cases be the cost to the employer, less any reimbursement by the employee.

The case of Pepper v. Hart, 1993, established that the cost of a benefit shall for tax purposes be based on the marginal, not average, cost. Marginal cost means essentially the additional cost to the employer for providing the benefit. It is likely that there will be problems in arriving at marginal cost and that some of these problems will be resolved by legislation or statements of Inland Revenue practice. Pepper v. Hart specifically concerned the benefit obtained by teachers who obtained places at reduced fees for their children in schools where the teachers were employed; in these cases the Inland Revenue has announced that no benefit will arise for payments of at least 15% of normal fees. Likewise it is accepted that the marginal cost of employees' travel in transport undertakings is nil where passengers paying normal fares are not displaced; and company goods sold to employees at not less than the wholesale price will not produce taxable benefits.

In the case of an asset placed at the disposal of a director, or employee earning more than £8,500, or members of their families, the cost is deemed to be the annual value of the benefit. The annual value of accommodation is the letting value.

From 5 April 1990, no tax has been charged on the benefit for employees earning more than £8,500 on nursery facilities provided by employers.

From 6 April 2005, the exemption for employer-supported childcare was widened to include other forms of employer-supported childcare and childcare vouchers in addition to workplace nurseries. Further details are available at www.hmrc.gov.uk/childcare.

Returns of benefits in kind for directors and higher-paid employees are made on form P11D, but for certain expenses a dispensation can be obtained from reporting on this form.

Business cars

(a) General. Taxpayers receive a benefit from the private use of business cars and this benefit is, in general, taxable; conversely, taxpayers can obtain tax allowances for the business use of their private cars. The treatment for tax purposes differs according to whether the taxpayer using the car is self-employed, an employee earning under £8,500 a year, a director or an employee earning £8,500 p.a. and above.

(b) Employees (not directors) earning under £8,500 p.a. No taxable benefit is chargeable for the use of a car provided by the employer, provided some use of the car is made for business. However, the figure of £8,500 includes all the potentially taxable benefits.

(c) Self-employed persons. From 2009/10 capital allowances are calculated by reference to a car's carbon dioxide emissions rather than cost. Where applicable, expense claims relating to the cost of fuel, maintenance, insurance and tax charged in the business accounts will need to be reduced for private use of the vehicle.

(d) Volunteer drivers. Volunteer drivers are liable for tax on any profit made on mileage allowances received from hospitals and similar volunteer organisations. The profit is the excess of the mileage allowances received over the Inland Revenue estimate of the cost per mile of running and maintaining the car.

(e) Car Benefits

* Taxable car benefit is calculated by multiplying the price of a car for tax purposes (essentially its list price plus accessories, less any capital contribution paid by the employee) by an appropriate percentage, graduated according to the car's level of CO_2 emissions.
* Cars with CO_2 emissions less than 75g/km have an appropriate percentage of 5%. For cars with emissions greater than 75g/km but less than 94g/km a rate of 11% applies to petrol-fuelled cars.
* Where the CO_2 emissions exceed 94g/km the benefit will increase by 1% for each 5 g/km of extra CO_2 emissions, subject to a maximum of 35% of list price. The exact CO_2 figure is rounded down to the nearest 5 g/km.
* Diesel cars are subject to a 3% supplement (subject to an overall maximum of 35%). It was announced in the 2013 Budget that the 3% supplement will

be removed from 2016/17.

- Cars with no CO2 emission or registered before 1 January 1998 are assessed by reference to their engine size.

Disabled drivers

The cost of converting a company car for use by a disabled person is no longer included in the price of the car for car benefit purposes.

Car fuel charges

Car fuel benefit charges are made in respect of employees receiving free fuel for private mileage in company cars.

The way in which the benefit is measured is directly linked to the CO2 emissions of the company car. The same percentage used to calculate car benefit is applied to calculate fuel benefit. This percentage is then multiplied against a set figure for the year. This set figure has been increased for 2014/15 to £21,700 (£21,100 for 2013/14).

The set percentages are increased by 3 points for diesel cars (subject to a maximum of 35%) and there are discounts for alternative fuelled cars.

No charge applies if the employee is required to make good to the employer the cost of *all* fuel used for private purposes and does, in fact, do so.

From 6 April 2007 to 5 April 2014, the taxable benefit for a van with unrestricted private use was £3,000, irrespective of the age of the van. The taxable benefit has been increased for 2014/15 to £3,090. In addition, where an employer provides fuel for unrestricted private use, an additional fuel charge of £581 will also apply (£564 for 2013/14).

When the van is unavailable for any part of the tax year, the chargeable benefit is reduced in proportion to the number of days in that year for which it was unavailable.

A van can be a car converted to carry goods or tools and equipment. This would be by the removal of the rear seats, seat belts, etc. It has to be incapable of being reconverted in less than an 'evening'.

There is no charge charge where a van is provided mainly for business use. Private use must be restricted to commuting with any other private use being insignificant. By way of example HMRC have indicated that insignificant private use would include such trips as an occasional trip to the tip or the local shop, but not regular supermarket shopping.

Company cars sold to employees. The employee may be liable for tax on the excess of the market value over the price at which the car is sold to him. This particularly applies to cars previously leased to customers.

Employees' transport – general rules. If an employee is necessarily obliged to use his own car on his employer's business, the employee can deduct the expenses of doing so from any reimbursement he receives from the employer. The reimbursement normally takes the form of a mileage rate. Any surplus which results is taxable in the employee's hands and a deficiency is a tax-allowable deduction from the employee's earnings. It is interesting to note that these rules also apply to the use of the employee's horse and bicycle at 20p per mile and motorcycle at 24p! It is, however, necessary to record and justify records of business and private mileage and of the expenses incurred, the expenses being apportioned on the basis of the proportionate business mileage. Obviously difficulties arise in keeping accurate records and for this reason the Authorised Mileage Rates Scheme, explained below, is easier to operate.

Cash alternative – When the use of a company car is readily convertible into cash by an employee who is a director or whose total earnings for the year including the benefit are £8,500 a year or more, the cash equivalent is chargeable to tax in the employee's hands. The employer is liable to pay Class 1A National Insurance contributions on the benefit (TA 1988 S.19). If the employee receives a higher salary instead of the use of a company car that employee will, in the normal course, be liable to tax on the higher salary. Even in the case where an option to take a higher salary is offered by the employer, the employee will pay tax on the option of the higher salary (*Heaton v Bell* 1969).

Authorised Mileage Rates – From 6 April 2002, a new system of flat rate mileage allowances was introduced for employees using their own transport for business journeys. Employers no longer need to report mileage payments up to their authorised rates, and dispensations will no longer apply.

The rates are as follows:

Cars and vans

First 10,000 miles in any tax year	45p per mile
Additional miles over 10,000	25p per mile
Motorcycles	24p per mile
Bicycles	20p per mile

From 6 April 2002 to 5 April 2010 the rate for the first 10,000 miles was 40p.

If the employee receives from the employer a mileage rate greater than the sum above, the employee will be taxed on the excess. Any deficit between the amount received and the above rates can be claimed against tax. Since 6 April 2002, no relief is available for interest on loans to buy the transport.

Gifts, gratuities and parties

In general, gifts are taxable in the hands of employees if they arise out of the employment. Typical examples of taxable gifts are tips, footballers' benefits and Christmas gifts. Gift vouchers are assessable at their cost to the employer, but luncheon vouchers for no more than 15p a day are not assessable; nor are meals in a canteen available for employees generally or long-service awards to employees up to £50 per year of service (up from £20 per year in 2002/03). Gifts to employees by third parties are not taxable up to £250 p.a., nor is entertainment provided by third parties. Modest expenditure on staff parties, e.g. at Christmas, is not regarded as a benefit if less than £150 per person. The expenditure, from 6 April 1995, may be spent on more than one event as long as the total is not exceeded. If one function costs more than £150 per head the whole amount is assessed. If more than £150 is spent on more than one event or function, it is those functions which take the expenditure over £150 and beyond which are assessable.

Gift aid

Charitable gifts by individuals and close companies qualify for tax relief. From 6 April 2000, there is no longer a minimum.

From 6 April 2000, the upper limit on gifts deducted from wages is abolished.

For gifts made under Gift Aid after 5 April 2003, donors may elect to have the donation treated as though made in the previous year of assessment.

From April 2004, taxpayers can nominate a charity to receive all or part of any tax repayment due to them. The nomination is made on the taxpayer's self-assessment form.

Accommodation

Where an employee is provided with a house or other accommodation rent-free or at a rent below the gross rateable annual value, he or she will normally be liable to pay tax on the annual value, reduced by the rent the employee pays. This does not apply to employees such as caretakers who are required to live in the accommodation as part of their duties, but the only directors who can obtain the advantage of this exemption are full-time working directors, or directors of non-profit-making companies, and they must have no material interest in the company. Accommodation provided for directors where there is a threat to their security is also exempt. The cost of heating, lighting, cleaning, repairs (other than structural repairs), maintenance, decoration, furniture and domestic effects, which is not met by the employee, must not exceed 10% of his or her emoluments.

Where an employee first occupies the house provided by his or her employers on and after 31 March 1983, and the cost of providing the accommodation exceeds £75,000, the employee may be liable for tax at the official rate of interest on the excess. Where the property has been held for six years before the employee's occupation, the cost becomes the market value with vacant possession.

From 1990/91 and onwards, companies cannot reclaim VAT on the provision of free accommodation for directors or their families.

Relocation: employees moving house

An employer may make a tax-free contribution of up to £8,000 for removal expenses of employees; the relief applies even if the employee retains the existing house, such as for letting. Relief for additional housing costs is withdrawn. The payments are not subject to PAYE but payments over £8,000 must be recorded by the employer on forms P9D or P11D.

Business expenses

In the case of directors, and employees earning more than £8,500, the expenses or expense allowances paid by the business are assessable on the individual. It is then necessary for the employee or director to satisfy the Inspector of Taxes that the expenses were incurred for the purpose of the business.

Relief is available on respect of certain incidental personal expenses paid by employers in respect of employees who are obliged to stay away from their homes overnight for business purposes. The most common such expenses include newspapers, telephone charges and laundry. The allowable amounts are £5 a night in the UK and £10 a night overseas. Payments above these limits are wholly chargeable to tax.

Beneficial loans

Where a loan is made by a business to an employee earning above £8,500, or a director, the individual will be chargeable to tax on the annual amount of interest below an 'official rate' to be notified by statutory instrument.

From 1994/95 to 2013/14, a tax exemption applied where an employee's cheap or interest-free loans totalled no more than £5,000. This exemption has been increased to £10,000 from 6 April 2014.

An employee may not be charged with tax on the benefit of cheap interest on a 'bridging loan' from his or her employer obtained because he or she had to change his residence owing to being transferred in the organisation. . This exemption is subject to restrictions and readers wishing to claim the exemption are advised to seek professional advice regarding the application of the rules to their individual circumstances.

Income tax is not payable by employees on loans from employers whose business includes the lending of money, provided the loan is made on the same terms as are available to the public, ignoring differences in initial fees of administration (FA 1994).

Home-working

The 2003 Budget included proposals to allow employers to contribute towards additional household costs incurred by an employee who works at home, some or all of the time, under agreed flexible working arrangements without it giving rise to a change to income tax.

Employers can pay up to £4 per week without the need for supporting evidence of the costs the employee incurred. Where the employer pays more than that amount, evidence is needed to show that the payment is wholly in respect of additional household expenses incurred by the employee in carrying out his duties at home.

Medical insurance

Where an employer pays an employee's medical expenses or pays premiums into a medical insurance scheme, there is a charge to tax. The benefit is the cost of the services/insurance less any contribution from the employee.

Statutory Maternity Pay (SMP)

Under the *Employee Protection Act 1975* maternity pay can be paid to an employee after the employee ceases to work due to pregnancy. These payments are taxable as income from employment if the contract of employment still exists, and tax is deducted. If the contract of employment has been terminated at the time of payment, tax is chargeable as other income, and the payments may be made gross.

Season tickets

The value of season tickets for travel to work provided by employers for employees is assessable on the employees, but loans made by employers for employees to buy season tickets are generally exempt.

Credit cards

The value of purchases under credit cards made payable and chargeable to employers is taxable in the hands of the employees.

Armed Forces leave travel

Warrants or allowances for leave travel by members of the armed forces are exempt from tax.

Employer-supported childcare

From 6 April 2005 to 5 April 2011, employees could receive up to £55 per week of childcare, free of tax and National Insurance, provided employers contracted with an approved childcarer or provided vouchers to pay an approved carer. To qualify, the benefit must have been available to all employees.

Employers are required to estimate the employee's likely annual earnings in the case of employees joining an employer-supported childcare scheme on or after 6 April 2011. For those employees whose expected level of earnings is between the basic and higher rate limits the tax free limit of childcare support will be £28 per week. In the case of employees with expected earnings in excess of the higher rate the exempt limit will be £25 per week (was £22 per week for 2012/13 when the additional rate of tax was 50%) and the exempt limit for those employees with earnings below the basic rate limit remains at £55 per week.

From the Autumn of 2015 parents will be able to buy childcare vouchers through an online scheme, whose cost will be subsidised by the Government at a rate of £20 for every £80 paid by the parent, up to a limit of £1,200 per child i.e. 20% of annual childcare costs up to a maximum of £6,000. The employer-provided system of childcare vouchers is to be phased out.

2.10 LIABILITY INSURANCE AND UNINSURED LIABILITIES

On and after 6 April 1995 liability insurance on work-related risks is tax-free for employees and gives tax relief when paid for by employers. The tax-free relief applies for 6 years after the end of the employment. Also tax-free are payments for uninsured work-related charges which could have been insured, and these charges could include legal costs in defending an action.

2.11 LIFE ASSURANCE

To 13 March 1984

Policies made up to this date, and not subsequently amended, provide relief from income tax by means of a deduction of 12.5% from 6 April 1989 (previously 15%) from the premium payments. For the purpose of this relief the premiums could not exceed the greater of one sixth of the taxpayer's net income after charges, or £1,500 in a tax year.

After 13 March 1984

The above relief is withdrawn for policies taken out after this date and for existing policies where the benefits are subsequently improved.

2.12   NATIONAL INSURANCE AND SOCIAL SECURITY

Details of the current National Insurance contributions and benefits are obtainable from various pamphlets issued by the Department of Social Security. Contributions are divided into four classes, as follows:

Class 1.	Employed persons
Class 2.	Self-employed persons
Class 3.	Voluntary contributions
Class 4.	Earnings-related contributions payable by the self-employed on earnings above a minimum, in addition to Class 2 contributions

The contributions do not give relief from income tax. Employers' contributions under Class 1 are, however, deductible charges in computing taxable profits. Class 1a contributions are made by employers who provide a range of benefits or refund expenses to directors and higher-paid employees. For a comprehensive guide, please see the excellent Inland Revenue guide on Class 1A (CWG5 – 2008).

The rates and thresholds are set out below.

	2014/15 £	2013/14 £
Lower earnings limit	£111 pw	£109 pw
Primary threshold	£153 pw	£149 pw
Secondary threshold	£153 pw	£148 pw
Employees' primary class 1 rate on earnings between primary threshold and upper earnings limit	12%	12%
Employees' primary class 1 rate on earnings above upper earnings limit	2%	2%
Upper earnings limit	£805 pw	£797 pw
Employers' secondary class 1 rate on earnings above secondary threshold	13.8%	13.8%
Lower profits limit (for self-employed Class 4 contribution)	£7,956	£7,755
Class 4 rate on profits between lower and upper profits limit	9%	9%
Class 4 rate on profits above upper profits limit	2%	2%

Social security benefits

(a) Taxable. The following benefits are taxable: retirement pension, widow's pensions and allowances; statutory sick pay (see below); statutory maternity pay; guardians and special allowances for children. The Job Seekers Allowance, excepting the earnings-related supplement and benefits to strikers' families, is taxable. Incapacity benefit is taxable except for the first 28 weeks and except where paid to persons receiving the former invalidity benefit at 12 April 1995 for the same incapacity

(b) Not taxable. The following benefits are not taxable: child benefit, benefits for sickness benefit (but not statutory sick pay), maternity, invalidity, industrial injury; mobility allowance; death grant; income support; housing credit; attendance allowance; family credit; supplementary benefits and pensions for wounds or disability payable to members of the armed forces, merchant seamen, and to civilians for war injury; war widows' pensions; and child dependency allowances. The Job Finder's grant is tax-free.

(c) Statutory sick pay (SSP). This is a payment which an employer is bound to make to most employees for absence due to sickness from 4 days to up to 28 weeks in a tax year. It forms part of the employee's income for tax and National Insurance purposes.

Employers do not require medical evidence before paying SSP.

Married women paying reduced rates of NI contributions are entitled to SSP.

The following are not entitled to SSP:

- Where other state benefits have been received
- Where the maximum entitlement of SSP has been received
- Those on strike.

In addition to the statutory entitlement to SSP an employee may be entitled to what is called 'occupational sick pay' (OSP) from the employer under his or her contract of service or custom in the employment. The rules of OSP may involve a deduction for SSP and state sickness benefits. Payments of OSP are also taxable in the employee's hands, except to the extent that the employee has contributed to a fund for the purpose.

The detailed rules for the calculation and eligibility for SSP can be complicated in particular cases and further information can be obtained from the Department of Social Security.

(d) Unemployment and strikes – Job Seeker's Allowance (JSA). The Job Seeker's Allowance, received by the unemployed person and one adult dependant (e.g. wife, husband, parent), is taxable and forms part of the taxpayer's total income for tax purposes in a tax year. Additions for children are not taxable.

Where the unemployment is prolonged, and the total income including JSA is consequently small, a refund of tax already paid (e.g. under PAYE) may be due. This would apply if the total income in a tax year to 5 April was below the personal and other allowances to which the taxpayer was entitled. This refund could not be obtained while benefit was being paid but would be paid soon after the next 5 April or, if the jobseeker enters employment prior to that date, possibly by way of an adjustment to the PAYE tax code.

As no tax is deducted from the benefits, and if the taxpayer's other income is sufficiently high, he or she might be liable for unpaid tax at the end of the tax year. This unpaid amount would be collected in the following tax year, usually by adjustment to the PAYE code if the taxpayer was then in employment.

Supplementary benefit for persons who do not have to make themselves available for employment is not taxable. Such persons include those over retirement age, single parents of children under 16, and those looking after disabled people.

JSA is one of a number of benefits due to be replaced by universal credit over the period from October 2013 to the end of 2017.

(e) Persons on strike. No benefit is payable to persons on strike, but supplementary benefit may be payable to a wife and this benefit is taxable. Tax is not deducted from the benefit. If any refund of tax is due it cannot be paid until the taxpayer returns to work, and if there is additional tax payable it will be recovered by adjustment to the taxpayer's PAYE coding for a future year. In all cases the tax payable for a tax year will be assessed soon after 5 April at the year end.

2.13 CHARITABLE GIVING

With effect from 6 April 2000, deeds of covenant were brought within the Gift Aid scheme. No Gift Aid declaration is required in respect of deeds of covenant executed before 6 April 2000.

One-off payments of any amount can be made to charities under the Gift Aid scheme, provided a Gift Aid declaration is made. Such a declaration may cover any number of donations already made or about to be made.

Declarations can be made in writing, by telephone, over the internet or orally – the essential point being that the charity obtains the donor's name and address.

Tax relief on Gift Aid is given at the payer's highest rate of tax. Basic rate relief is given by the donor deducting tax at source. Higher rate relief is given by extending the basic rate band by the gross amount of the payment.

Example:

Mr A makes a payment of £80 to charity. He is a higher rate taxpayer. For 2014/15, Mr A's basic rate will be extended to an upper earnings limit of £31,865 + (£80 x 100/80) = £31,965. The gross payment of £100 is not deducted in calculating Statutory Total Income.

Income tax relief is also available in respect of gifts of shares to charity. Such shares must be listed on a recognised stock exchange. The donor may deduct 'the relevant amount' from his income in calculating Statutory Total Income. The relevant amount is the market value of the shares at the date of the gift.

2.14   INTEREST PAID AND HOME LOANS

Summary

In general, interest payable by an individual on a debt or a loan, including hire purchase and overdraft interest, is not an allowable charge against his or her income for tax purposes. However, interest paid does give tax relief in the following cases: loans for business purposes; purchase of retirement annuities where the loan is charged on property; and letting of residential accommodation. These cases are considered briefly below.

Loans for business

Interest paid is an allowable expense where the loan is used for business purposes, including the interest on hire purchase transactions. Interest is also allowable in the following special cases:

- Loans for buying shares in partnership or loans to the partnership; this also applies to co-operatives. The borrower need not be an active member of the partnership.

- Loans for acquiring ordinary shares in close companies or for loans to close companies (excluding investment companies). A close company is one controlled by five or less 'participators', meaning generally shareholders. The participator, his or her relatives and associates (e.g. partners), count as one person for this purpose. To qualify the borrower must either (i) own more than 5% of the ordinary shares in the company, or (ii) own some shares and work full-time in the company.

- Loans for enabling employees to acquire ordinary shares in an employee-controlled company. The employee or his or her spouse must work full-time in the company. The company must be resident in the UK, must be a trading company and 'unquoted', i.e. there is no quotation for its shares on a Stock Exchange, and 75% of its ordinary shares, and the voting power, must be in the hands of the employees or their spouses. Other conditions apply.

The relief is withdrawn where the entity of the borrower changes, except where the loan could have been treated as a new loan to the new business entity.

Loans to buy retirement annuities

Tax relief is available on interest on the first £30,000 of a pre 9 March 1999 loan to a borrower aged 65 or more to purchase a life annuity, the loan being secured on the borrower's home.

Loans for let property

Relief on the interest is available provided that the property is let for at least 26 weeks in a year at a commercial rent.

Loans to directors and higher-paid employees

Where directors and employees earning over £8,500 a year receive loans from their employers of more than £10,000 in total at interest rates below a commercial rate the saving in interest is treated as a benefit and taxable as earnings from employment.

2.15   MAKING PROVISION FOR RETIREMENT

Introduction

The main ways of providing funds for retirement are:

- State Pension
- company/occupational pension schemes
- personal pension schemes
- retirement annuity schemes.

Most UK individuals will be entitled to some form of State Pension when they retire. However, the growing cost of the state scheme has been a cause for concern and legislation has been introduced in recent years to equalise pensionable ages for men and women and to raise the pensionable age. Currently, basic State Pension is available, depending on their dates of birth, to men between the ages of 65 and 68 and women between the ages of 60 and 65.

The State Pension is funded from National Insurance Contributions. It is paid gross and is taxable.

It is generally recognised that relying solely on State Pension to fund one's retirement is unlikely to provide sufficient income and increasing efforts are being made to persuade people to put aside additional funds during their working lives to provide additional income when they retire. The most common ways of doing this are by making contributions to occupational pension schemes provided by employers or by personal pension schemes. Retirement annuity schemes were introduced before personal pension schemes. Taxpayers with existing retirement annuity schemes can continue to pay into such schemes, but no new schemes can be set up.

Readers should note that what follows is a general overview of the pension regime focusing mainly on an individual making pension provision. A more detailed explanation of the new regime can be found in the latest edition of *Pensions Simplified* published by Management Books 2000 Limited.

The New Pension Regime

The former complex requirements for obtaining approval for pension schemes have been replaced by a simpler process of scheme registration. This allows schemes to obtain tax privileges whereby they will generally not be liable to pay tax on income and gains.

Annual limit for relief

Individuals who are active members of registered pension schemes are entitled to tax relief on contributions paid during a tax year. The maximum amount of contributions on which tax relief can be obtained in any one tax year is the higher of £3,600 or the individual's UK relevant earnings for that year.

UK relevant earnings are:

- Employment income
- Trading income (including income from furnished holiday lets)
- Patent income in relation to inventions

There is no earnings cap as was the case before 6 April 2006 but taxpayers should have regard to the *annual allowance* when calculating the level of contributions they wish to make in anyone tax year.

Tax relief on contributions can be given in one of three ways.

(i) Where schemes are administered by employers, contributions are deducted from employment income before tax (known as the 'net pay arrangements').

(ii) Individuals may obtain basic rate tax relief at source. If, for example, an individual wished to increase his personal pension fund by £1,000 in 2014/15, he would pay £800 to the pension fund. The remaining £200 would be added by the pension fund administrator making a claim to HM Revenue & Customs. Higher rate tax relief is given by extending an individual's basic rate tax band by the amount of the gross contribution. (It should be noted that as from 6 April 2006, relief is only given for contributions paid in the tax year. There is no longer any provision to allow contributions to be back-dated to previous tax years. However, any unused annual allowance for up to three tax years preceding 'the current tax year' may be added to the current tax year. The earliest years' unused allowance is used first (See below for a description of. The annual allowance was reduced from £50,000 in 2013/14 to £40,000 from 6 April 2014. For the purpose of calculating unused annual allowance the current limit of £40,000 is used even for years ending on or before 5 April 2014.)

(iii)   In exceptional cases, relief may be given by making a claim. For example, this method of relief applies to contributions to existing retirement annuity contracts. In these cases, relief is given by way of the pension contributions being deducted from relevant earnings in the year of payment.

Annual allowance

The term *annual allowance* refers to the amount by which existing pension savings in a registered pension scheme are permitted to grow each year free of tax. Increases over and above the annual allowance are subject to an annual allowance tax charge of 40%, the charge being payable by the individual member.

It should be noted that pension growth can be by way of contributions made during the year or via growth in the capital value of the fund.

The incoming Coalition Government announced its intention to effectively repeal the changes introduced by the previous Government in the 2009 Budget. On 14 October 2010 new restrictions were announced. The annual allowance for 2011/12 onwards was significantly reduced to £50,000 (2010/11 £255,000) and the lifetime allowance (see below) is reduced from £1.5m to £1.25m from 2014/15. From 2014/15 the annual allowance has been further reduced to £40,000. However, relief for contributions to a registered pension scheme will continue to be given at an individual's marginal rate of tax (20%,40% or 45%).

Lifetime allowance

Retirement funds which have been set up to provide benefits are also subject to a lifetime allowance. The lifetime allowance was reduced to £1.25m for 2014/15 (£1.5m 2013/14).

A lifetime allowance charge will be levied where pension funds have been built up and the capital value exceeds the lifetime allowance. The charge will be triggered by a *'benefit crystallisation event'* such as when payments are made from the retirement fund by way of a pension or a lump sum. It is calculated on the amount crystallised to the extent that payments from the fund exceed the lifetime allowance at the date of the benefit crystallisation event. The charge is set at 25% (55% in the case of lump sums). Generally, the scheme administrator will deduct the relevant tax from the fund and pay it over to HM Revenue & Customs.

Retirement benefits

Currently, benefits must be taken at age 75 at the latest, but the Government announced in the 2014 Budget that, from 2015/16, individuals with defined contribution pension plans will be able to draw all their pension savings at retirement without restriction, although such withdrawals will be taxable at their marginal rate of tax (after deducting any tax free element of such withdrawals). Individuals who choose to draw all their pension savings will not have to purchase an annuity at that point. In the transition period the rules regarding drawdown are being relaxed. The minimum pension age currently is set at 55.

Pension income taken from registered pension schemes is subject to income tax. It should be noted that it is not necessary to retire before drawing pension benefits.

Transitional provisions

Approved pension schemes in existence immediately before 6 April 2006 were deemed to be registered schemes for the purpose of the new regime.

Transitional rules provided two types of protection for existing members of pension schemes in relation to the lifetime allowance charge. *Primary protection* assists individuals with pension rights in excess of £1.5m at 6 April 2006. The lifetime allowance for such individuals was increased by the excess of the pre-commencement pension rights over the standard lifetime allowance.

Enhanced protection applied to individuals who ceased active membership of a pension scheme before 6 April 2006, provided they did not subsequently become active members of any other registered scheme. Such individuals were not generally subject to a lifetime allowance charge, however large their retirement fund was.

3

Savings Income

General

For individuals with taxable income below the basic rate threshold of £31,865 in 2014/15 (£32,010 in 2013/14), most investment income is charged to tax at 20% except for dividend income, which carries a tax credit of 10% of the gross dividend. Basic rate taxpayers have no further tax to pay in respect of such income.

Taxpayers whose income exceeds £31,865 but is less than £150,000 are chargeable to tax at 40% on non-dividend savings income and 32.5% on dividend income. They therefore have further tax to pay of 20% on non-dividend savings income and 22.5% on dividend income. Where interest is received gross, there will be further tax to pay of 40%.

For taxpayers whose income exceeds £150,000 in 2014/15 or 2013/14 the tax rates are 45% on non-dividend income and £37.5% on dividend income. Such taxpayers would have further tax to pay of 25% on non-dividend income and 27.5% on dividend income.

We now move on to consider specific types of savings income in more detail.

Starting rate of 10% on savings income for low earners

In the case of savings income other than dividends, there is a starting rate of 10%, applicable on savings income up to £2,880 (2013/14 £2,790), *provided that* non-savings income will be accounted for BEFORE savings income in determining whether this threshold has been exceeded. In other words, if total non-savings income exceeds the amount of the personal allowance, the amount of savings income chargeable at 10% will reduce progressively, down to zero when total non-savings income exceeds the amount of the personal allowance plus £2,880. It can be seen, therefore, that the 10% rate applies only to people with relatively low non-savings income.

From 6 April 2015, the starting rate will be reduced to 0% and the savings band will increase to £5,000.

Taxed interest

Subject to the exceptions indicated below, interest received by the taxpayer is normally a net amount after the payer has deducted tax at the 20% rate. It includes interest received on company debentures, most government securities, local authority loans, other loans and deposits in building societies and banks. The taxpayer must enter the gross amount before tax on the return of income and it is the gross amount which forms part of the total income for the purpose, for example, of calculating any liability to higher-rate tax. If the taxpayer is not liable to tax or if the taxpayer's top rate of tax is the 10% band and they have suffered tax at 20% on interest received, they can recover the excess.

Untaxed interest

This refers to interest received without deduction of tax and would include interest from National Savings, government stock on the National Savings and Trustee Savings Bank registers, and 3½% War Loan. Tax is payable by assessment on untaxed interest, but it is particularly suitable for those not liable to tax, including charities. Individuals who are not liable for income tax can apply for interest to be paid gross. From 6 April 1996 tax on these sources is only charged at 20% if any tax is due.

Taxed dividends

From 1999/00, dividends from UK companies carry a tax credit equal to 1/9th of the dividend (representing 10% of the gross dividend including the tax credit), but the tax credit cannot be reclaimed if the individual's total tax liability is less than the tax credit. The 10% tax credit will continue to satisfy the tax liability at lower and basic rates. Higher rate taxpayers will have an effective rate of 32.5% if their taxable income is between £31,865 and £150,000, or 37.5% if their taxable income is greater than £150,000.

Dividends and interest from overseas

The tax deducted or imputed may include overseas tax as well as the UK basic rate. The latter deduction may be lower as a result of double taxation relief.

Dividends paid by close companies

Business owners can opt to take a part of their remuneration in the form of dividends. It is currently common for directors of small limited companies to take their remuneration by way of a relatively small salary (to secure state pension rights) with the balance of remuneration taken by way of dividends (thereby obtaining a saving in employer's and employee's National Insurance.) There are, however, a number of traps for the unwary and readers contemplating a change in their remuneration package would be well advised to seek professional guidance before taking any action.

Note that dividends can only be paid out of 'distributable reserves' – the company must have made a cumulative profit, and paid corporation tax on it, before a dividend can be paid.

Accrued interest

In the case of interest-bearing marketable securities such as government stocks, most local authority and company loan stock, the amount of investment income for tax purposes includes accrued interest added to the price on their sale. This would be the case, for example, where the buyer receives a payment of interest which covers the period before the purchase. On the other hand, if the sale was made close to the date when interest was payable, the seller would receive the interest and the proportion due to the buyer would be deducted from the price. Accrued interest is chargeable to tax only where the total nominal value of the securities owned by the taxpayer is above £5,000.

Likewise manufactured dividends are taxable. These represent payments to compensate buyers of securities for loss of dividend due, for instance, to late delivery of purchased shares.

Deep gain securities

Tax is payable on the discount obtained from deep gain securities when the amount payable on the redemption of a bond exceeds the issue price by more than ½% per annum or 15% in total and when the timing and amount of the redemption is uncertain. The income tax payable reduces the capital gains tax payable on the redemption of the securities. The rules do not apply where redemption can be enforced on the default (e.g. insolvency) of the issuer.

Capital gains

For treatment of capital gains and the inheritance tax in respect of investment see Chapters 5 and 9 of this book.

3.2   PERSONAL EQUITY PLANS (PEPS)

The PEP scheme was a government sponsored savings scheme which offered investors a number of tax advantages on qualifying investments. With effect from 6 April 1999 the PEP scheme was discontinued, and investors were encouraged to transfer PEP investments into an Individual Savings Account (ISA). For those who still hold their original PEP investments, the relief from capital gains tax on disposal continues to apply. However the income tax advantages of PEP funds, whereby the finds could reclaim dividend tax credits from HMRC, no longer apply.

3.3 INTEREST RECEIVABLE

General

Interest receivable forms part of the total income of all taxpayers, including individuals, companies and other bodies liable to tax. In most cases income tax at 20% is deducted, or assumed to be deducted, by the payer, and this system applies with some exceptions to government securities, debentures, other quoted stock and loans generally. If the recipient of the interest is not liable to pay tax the amount deducted can be reclaimed from the Inland Revenue. From 6 April 1999, if the top band is 10%, the difference can be reclaimed. Claims for repayment of tax at £50 or over can be made before the end of the year.

Interest gross of tax

In the following cases the interest is receivable without deduction of tax:

- on National Savings accounts – see below
- from the Post Office
- on offshore accounts, e.g. those in the Isle of Man and the Channel Islands, and when received by persons not ordinarily resident in the UK
- when application is made (on form R85) by a non-taxpayer for bank and building society interest to be paid gross. Severe penalties apply to false declarations.

Basis of assessment

Tax is now based on the amount of interest received in the tax year.

Payment of tax on interest

In most cases the taxpayer's liability for lower and basic rate tax on interest received will be satisfied by deduction of tax from the payment, the payer having to account to the Inland Revenue for the tax so deducted. Where interest is paid gross, the taxpayer is liable to pay tax on the interest on 31 January following the year of assessment. However, for employees and pensioners the tax liability is usually met by the appropriate deduction from the allowances given in the coding. This adjustment to the coding is normally estimated so that a further coding adjustment may be necessary when the actual interest is known, or a refund of tax may be due.

For the purpose of calculating the taxpayer's liability to higher rate tax interest paid net of tax will be grossed up, and the excess over the basic rate will be payable on 31 January following the end of the year of assessment.

National Savings

(a) Ordinary Accounts. The National Savings and Investments Ordinary Account is no longer on sale, and all existing accounts are now closed for transactions. Ordinary accounts have been replaced by Easy Access Savings Accounts.

(b) Investment Account. A higher rate of interest is payable than on the ordinary account but the interest is taxable, although tax is not deducted at source. Attractive to charities and individuals not liable to tax (who can apply for interest to be paid gross). One month's notice is required for withdrawal.

(c) National Savings Certificates and National Savings Bonds. A variety of issues have been made with tax-free interest.

(d) Save as You Earn. This product is no longer available. It was a system by which the saver contracted to make regular monthly contributions from £5 up to £150 a month to the National Savings Bank, the Trustee Savings Bank, other banks or certain building societies. A bonus, payable after certain stated periods, was tax free. At the end of three years savers had the option of taking the amount accrued in cash or buying shares in their company at a price set three years earlier, and this price could be discounted by up to 20%. Anyone who has previously invested in a Save as You Earn plan from National Savings and Investments should consider reinvesting or cashing in their investments as many of the issues are no longer earning interest.

(e) Premium Savings Bonds. The maximum holding is £30,000 and prize money is tax-free.

(f) Children's Bonds. Children's Bonus Bonds from National Savings and Investments allow taxpayers to invest tax-free for their child's future in their own name. All returns on Children's Bonus Bonds are completely tax-free for both child and parent.

(g) National Savings Pensioners Guaranteed Income Bond. These bonds are no longer on sale. They were available to people aged 60 and over from 29 November 1995 and paid monthly interest at fixed rates guaranteed for one, two or five years.

Savings with friendly societies

Unlike mainstream life assurance companies, friendly societies are still able to offer tax-exempt life assurance policies, subject to strict conditions. The maximum annual premium is £270, and the tax-exempt surrender value is payable out of a tax-exempt fund after 10 years (or 7½ years for certain shorter-term policies) and need not be limited to a return of the premiums. These policies can represent tax-efficient forms of saving, especially for children under the age of 18.

3.4 INDIVIDUAL SAVINGS ACCOUNTS (ISAs)

This is a savings vehicle designed to make more people save. Its stated aim is to help the poor save. From 6 April 1999, it replaced new PEPs and TESSAs.

Changes were brought in from 6 April 2005, and the main details are currently as follows.

- The tax benefits are guaranteed to last for at least 10 years.
- The returns are free from tax.
- There is no statutory minimum holding period or minimum subscription level.
- Qualifying investments are in 2 groups:
  - bank and building society accounts, and National Savings products
  - stocks and shares.
- For 6 April 2014 to 30 June 2014 the ISA investment limits are £11,880 of which up to £5,940 can be saved in cash. In 2013/14 the investment limits were £11,520 and £5,760 respectively.
- From 1 July 2014, Individual Savings Accounts (ISAs) will be called 'New ISAs' (NISAs). The annual subscription limit will be increased to £15,000 and the current rule whereby only half of the overall annual limit can go into a cash ISA will be abolished. Investors will also be allowed to transfer their investments from a stocks and shares account to a cash account.
- Junior ISAs were introduced with effect from 1 November 2011. They are available to UK resident children under the age of 18 who do not have a Child Trust Fund account. When the holder reaches the age of 18, a junior ISA becomes an adult ISA. The annual amount that can be invested in a Junior ISA or Child Trust Fund account will rise to £4,000 from 1 July 2014.

Other facts:

- One company can run all aspects of the ISA (maxi) for an individual, or alternatively different companies (mini) can run the respective cash and stocks separately.
- Cash can be withdrawn any time without penalty but cannot be replaced if

the cash limit was already reached previously.
- No lifetime limit applies.
- Shares from de-mutualised companies cannot be bought into an ISA.
- New 'stakeholder' cash and medium-term products can be held with ISAs.

3.5 PROFIT SHARING

General

Companies operate various schemes allowing their employees, including directors, to obtain shares and share in profits in those companies on favourable terms. The employees may be offered options to acquire shares at below market prices; they may obtain the shares through Save As You Earn contracts; they may obtain interests in shares through trusts set up for the purpose; or they may be allotted shares individually. The profit-related pay schemes initiated in 1987 have now been phased out. Many conditions apply to all these schemes for tax purposes but the general effect of the legislation is outlined as follows.

Share options

Where an option is granted to a director or employee by reason of an office or employment there will generally be a charge to tax not when the option is granted, but when it is exercised. The charge will then be on the difference between the value received and the amount paid (both for the shares and for the option itself). Liability to tax on the option can be avoided if the option is granted under one of the HMRC-approved share option schemes.

SAYE share option scheme

This scheme gives employees the right to buy shares at a fixed price, using the proceeds of SAYE (Save As You Earn) savings contracts. The price of the shares will be fixed at the time the option is granted, and the price must not be less than 80% of the market value of the shares at that time.

Employees do not have to use their options – this will depend on whether the shares increase in value over the period of the savings contract. If they do not use their options they will still receive the proceeds of their SAYE contract (tax free) when the contract matures.

Under the SAYE contract, the employee saves a regular amount between £5 and £250 per month for 3, 5 or 7 years. The savings will stop after the contract period, but the contract may provide for the savings, plus bonus, to be paid.

A scheme will only be approved by HM Revenue and Customs if the shares used satisfy certain conditions to ensure that they are ordinary shares, and if the scheme is made available to all employees under similar terms.

If the scheme is approved the employee will not pay any income tax on:

- the granting of an option to buy shares at a favourable price
- any increase in the value of the shares between the date the option was given and the date on which it is exercised.

When the shares are sold any profit may still be charged to capital gains tax.

Company share option plans

This scheme provides similar tax reliefs to the SAYE Share Option Scheme. However, it is not linked to a savings contract, and, crucially, does not have to be operated for all employees on similar terms.

To qualify for tax reliefs, the option must be held for at least 3 and no more than 10 years, and only one option exercise can qualify for relief in any 3-year period. The scheme must also be approved by the Inland Revenue before any options are granted under it.

Only full-time directors (i.e. working 25 hours a week or more) and employees working at least 20 hours per week can participate, and there are limits on the size of options which can be granted. The maximum value of shares a person can have under option at any time is £30,000.

An individual cannot participate in a scheme if he has had a material interest in the share capital of the company in the previous 12 months. A material interest means owning or controlling more than 25% of the ordinary share capital or rights to more than 25% of the assets on a winding up.

Profit sharing through shares

The purpose of such schemes is to encourage employee participation in company profits by offering tax concessions on qualifying shareholdings; these tax concessions include freedom from income tax on employees' receipt of the shares, and freedom from capital gains tax on disposal. To qualify, the company must set up a trust fund which then purchases or subscribes shares and holds them in trust for the employees. In addition certain rules and conditions must be satisfied.

Prior to 6 April 2001, the scheme had to be available to all qualifying employees on similar terms. The shares could not generally be taken out of the trust for two years, and for the acquisition of the shares to be completely free of tax, the shares could not be taken out until after five years. There were complex rules on the operation of the scheme, on the types of shares which could be used, and on the maximum amount which could be allocated to each employee.

From 6 April 2001 onwards the old scheme was replaced by the 'share incentive plan' scheme referred to in the next section. People who hold shares allotted to them under the previous scheme still enjoy the same relief from capital gains tax on disposal.

Share incentive plans

- Employers can give employees up to £3,000 of shares each year free of tax and National Insurance.
- Some or all of these shares can be awarded to employees for reaching performance targets.
- Employees will be able to buy partnership shares out of their pre-tax salary up to a maximum of £1,500 a year, free of tax and National Insurance. Employees who keep their shares in the plan for 5 years will pay no income tax or National Insurance in respect of these shares.
- If the shares are only kept in the plan for 3 years, tax and National Insurance is paid on the initial value – any increase being tax free.
- If the employees retain the shares in the plan until disposal, they will not be liable to Capital Gains Tax.
- Companies will get corporation tax relief on costs they incur in providing shares for employees to buy, to the extent that such costs exceed the employee's contributions.
- Up to £1,500 of dividends may be reinvested in shares tax free each year within the trust.
- Employees and trustees will have freedom to make their own arrangements about transferring shares when an employee leaves.
- There is a new capital gains tax rollover relief to existing shareholders who want to sell their shares to a new plan trust to be used for the benefit of employees.
- The existence of arrangements to enable employees to sell shares in a new plan trust will not of itself make those shares readily convertible into cash, requiring the employers to operate PAYE and account for National Insurance.

Companies can send in draft plans for approval under a fast-track approvals system.

Enterprise Management Incentive Scheme

- Independent trading companies with gross assets not exceeding £30 million can award key employees with tax advantaged share options. An employee is not permitted to hold unexercised options in respect of shares with a total value of more than £250,000 at the time the options were granted. The shares that may be acquired under the scheme must be fully paid, irredeemable ordinary shares and the option must be capable of being exercised within 10 years from the date it is granted and must be non-transferable.

- There is no tax charge on the grant of the option and there will be normally no tax or National Insurance for the employee to pay when the options are exercised; nor will there normally be any National Insurance charge for the employer.
- The total value of the shares for which there are unexercised share options must not exceed £3 million.

3.6 ENTERPRISE INVESTMENT SCHEME (EIS)

This investment scheme replaced the Business Expansion Scheme on 1 January 1994 when the latter terminated in December 1993. The main features of the scheme are as follows:

- Unquoted trading companies trading but not necessarily resident or incorporated in the UK can from 6 April 1998 raise capital by issuing shares under the scheme subject to gross assets being less than £15 million before the investment and £16 million after. For shares in investee companies that are issued on or after 6 April 2012, the maximum annual combined amount that can be invested in any one company under the EIS or Venture Capital Trust (See 3.7 below) schemes is to be increased from £2 million to £5 million.
- Investors can subscribe for EIS shares up to £1,000,000 from 6 April 2012 (previously £500,000). This limit is available to both husband and wife. As from 2012/13 there is no minimum investment in the shares (previously £500).
- The investment in an EIS scheme gives tax relief at 30% from 6 April 2011 (previously 20%) and capital gains tax exemption on the first disposal of the shares. The shares must be held for three years (five years for shares issued before 6 April 2000).
- Qualifying investors must not be employees or shareholders of the company owning more than 30% of the shares, but subsequent to the issue of the shares an investor can become a paid director, retaining the right to the tax relief.
- Changes were announced in the 2009 Budget in relation to the extent to which investors are able to claim to have part of the investment treated as if the shares were issued in the previous year. From 6 April 2006 to 5 April 2009, half the investment made between 6 April and 5 October in any year, up to a maximum of £50,000, could be carried back to the previous tax year. Both these restrictions (the 50% limit and the absolute limit of

£50,000) were removed by the Finance Bill 2009 so that for 2009/10 and subsequent years the only limit is the overriding limit that tax relief is calculated by reference to a maximum £1,000,000 subscription in any one year.

3.7   VENTURE CAPITAL TRUSTS

VCTs provide a means whereby taxpayers can invest indirectly in unquoted shares and obtain similar tax reliefs to those available to investors in EIS shares. Individuals aged 18 or over who subscribe for new eligible shares in a VCT can claim income tax relief at 30% of the amount invested up to the lower of:

(i)   the maximum investment of £200,000 per tax year, or
(ii)   the individual's tax liability for the year in which the investment takes place.

Dividends received by individuals in respect of ordinary shares in a VCT are exempt from income tax subject to certain conditions. If an individual disposes of his or her shares within three years of their issue, VCT income tax investment relief is withdrawn.

Gains arising on the disposal of VCT shares are exempt from capital gains tax providing the original investments were within the qualifying limits referred to above. This applies to VCT shares purchased and those acquired by subscription.

3.8   SCRIP DIVIDENDS

Where a taxpayer opts to take a dividend in the form of shares or stock, instead of cash, the dividend will be grossed up at the dividend rate of income tax (10%). The gross amount will be chargeable to the higher rate of income tax (32.5%) if applicable. The market value may apply if higher than the cash equivalent.

The capital gains tax cost of such shares is, however, the net amount, not the grossed up equivalent.

3.9   UNIT TRUSTS

Authorised unit trusts and investment trusts have been exempt from capital gains tax on the trusts' investments since 31 January 1980. In the case of those trusts with specific instructions as to their operations, income from investment in gilt-edged stock is liable to basic rate income tax and not corporation tax.

In all cases, investors in the trusts will be liable to capital gains tax on the disposal of their holdings, subject to normal exemptions, and are also liable to income tax on dividends received. Regulations under the Charities Act 1992, effective on 1 January 1993, enable charitable unit trusts to transmit income to participating charities without deduction of tax.

When authorised under company law, open-ended investment companies (OEIC) will fall under the same provisions as apply to unit trusts. Open-ended investment companies are those where their shares are continuously created or redeemed.

3.10 OFFSHORE FUNDS

The offshore funds legislation applies to a wide range of investment vehicles set up overseas, often in the form of open-ended investment companies or unit trusts. If a significant proportion of the income is distributed to investors, the capital gains on the disposal of the investment is liable to capital gains tax. Where capital gains are rolled up in the fund the investors are charged income tax on the disposal of their holdings.

3.11 SEED ENTERPRISE INVESTMENT SCHEME

Provisions were included in the *Finance Act 2012* to introduce a new type of tax-advantaged venture capital scheme. The scheme is similar to the Enterprise Investment Scheme, but concentrated on smaller companies in the early stages of development. SEIS will run alongside EIS. The scheme was originally intended to be temporary and to run up to 6 April 2017, but it was announced in the 2014 Budget that the scheme is to be made permanent. The main features of the scheme are as follows:

- Income tax relief is available for investment in SEIS companies. These companies are defined as having no more than 25 employees and assets of up to £200,000 that are carrying on, or preparing to carry on, a new qualifying business.

- Tax relief is limited to 50% of the amount invested in new subscriber shares up to a limit of £100,000 per individual investor. It will be possible to carry back relief to the preceding year. Investors will not be entitled to relief if they own more than 30% of the voting share capital of the company.

- The shares must be retained for at least 3 years.

- Any one company will be permitted to raise up to £150,000 under the SEIS rules, this being a cumulative limit not an annual one.

- Chargeable gains on the disposal of SEIS shares will be exempt from CGT provided they have been held for 3 years prior to disposal. Qualifying investors can shelter other chargeable gains realised in 2012/13 and 2013/14 if they are re-invested in SEIS shares. A qualifying investor is essentially one who has no control over the issuing company or a subsidiary and no more than a 30% interest in the share capital, voting power or assets on a winding up of those companies in the period from the date of incorporation of the issuing company to 3 years after the date the shares were issued. Moreover, the investor must not be an employee of the issuing company or a subsidiary during the three year period from the date of issue of the shares. Directors are not excluded from relief, provided they do not have a substantial interest.

The scheme also includes many of the existing requirements of EIS such as the definitions of what constitutes a qualifying trading activity for the purposes of securing the tax relief.

3.12   SOCIAL INVESTMENT RELIEF

The 2014 Budget 2014 introduced a new income tax relief for investments by individuals in qualifying social enterprises after 5 April 2014. For the purposes of this tax relief 'social enterprise' means a community interest company, a community benefit society or a charity. The relief is given by way of a deduction from the investor's income tax liability equal to 30% of the amount invested. The maximum amount qualifying for relief is £1m per tax year and the investment must be held for at least 3 years. In order to qualify for relief the investment must take the form of subscriptions for shares in the social enterprise or a loan made to the enterprise meeting the conditions laid down in the *Finance Act 2014*.

Capital gains on social enterprise investments to which income tax relief applies will be exempt from capital gains tax provided the investments are held for at least 3 years. As with the EIS Scheme, a claim may be made for all or any part of a chargeable gain on the disposal of any asset to be deferred to the extent that it is matched by a qualifying investment in a social enterprise within one year before and three years after the disposal.

4

Business Taxation

4.1 THE SYSTEM SUMMARISED

The assessment

The profits from trading and professional activities are assessed as a separate source of income.

Strictly speaking, none of the personal reliefs and allowances reviewed in the previous chapters of this book is applicable to a business assessment as such. But where the business is unincorporated, i.e. owned by one person or a partnership, the reliefs and allowances applicable to the owners may be set off against their share of the business assessment. A limited company is, however, a 'legal person' and the tax assessment made on its own profits is not subject to the reliefs due to the owners, that is the shareholders, even if it is effectively owned by one person.

Unincorporated businesses and partnerships

The profits of a business owned by one individual or a partnership are liable to income tax. The amount so payable may be reduced by the owners' reliefs and allowances. It may be, however, that all of an individual taxpayer's reliefs are set off against income other than the profits from his or her business, and this situation should normally occur where the taxpayer was in a salaried employment as well as running a business. In the case of a partnership a return of the partnership computation must be made on behalf of the firm and the individual partners must make returns of their own incomes, including that received from the partnership. The tax payable is due by the individual partners in the agreed profit-sharing ratios.

From 6 April 2013 the Government introduced an optional cash basis of accounting for unincorporated businesses. For 2014/15 the cash basis is open to businesses whose turnover is less than £81,000 (£79,000 in 2013/14). These rules are aimed at unrepresented small businesses whose owners wish to make claims for tax credits. The rules aim to simplify reporting of income for the purposes of establishing entitlement to the new universal credit due to be implemented between October 2013 and December 2017. See section 4.5 for more details.

Incorporated businesses

So far as most limited companies and many other corporate bodies are concerned, their taxable profits are subject to corporation tax and not income tax.

Funds must be kept available for the payment of the tax liability nine months after the company's year end.

The dividend in the hands of the shareholder comes with a non-refundable tax credit at 10%.

Whether the business is incorporated or not the profits which it shows in its accounts will almost always need adjustment for the purpose of arriving at the profit figure on which tax is payable. This aspect of the subject is considered in the next section.

4.2   ADJUSTING THE ACCOUNTS PROFIT

General – the basis of adjustment

The profits shown in the accounts of a business, whether it is incorporated or not, are adjusted for tax purposes (a) by adding back expenses disallowed, and (b) by deducting income which is not taxable. The resulting assessment may then be reduced by capital allowances, and loss relief. The question as to whether a particular item is allowable or not is sometimes difficult to determine, and is a frequent cause of appeal to the Commissioners and to the Courts. For profits arising from trading, the over-riding rules are that expenditure must (a) be wholly and exclusively incurred for the purpose of the trade or profession, and (b) not be of a capital nature.

Over recent years attempts have been made to bring accounting practices and tax assessments closer into alignment so that accounting figures may be accepted as being those used for tax purposes. Whilst it is debatable whether or not this can ever be fully achieved, it is likely that further modifications to accounting practices and assessment procedures will be made in future to bring them still further into alignment. The option to elect for the new cash based system of accounting introduced with effect from 6 April 2013 continues this trend. See section 4.5 for more details.

Expenses disallowed

The following expenses are not allowed in the tax computation – that is, they must be added back to the accounts profits or deducted from an accounts loss:

- Expenses not arising out of the trade or profession, e.g. medical fees.
- Withdrawals of capital and profits, e.g. by dividends, proprietors' or partners' shares of profit or salaries (but salaries payable to directors of limited companies are normally allowable).

- Capital expenditure, such as extensions or improvements to premises, legal expenses connected with capital expenditure, company formation expenses, and capital losses. (Such expenses may, however, be allowable for capital gains tax purposes when the relevant assets are disposed of.)
- Depreciation. (As an alternative to accounting depreciation, there is a separate procedure for writing down assets for tax purposes – see 4.4 Capital Allowances.)
- Personal expenditure of proprietors such as personal life insurance premiums and private usage of business cars.
- Annual payments from which tax has been deducted, where the business is unincorporated and pays income tax.
- Appropriations of profit such as dividends, reserves and taxation.
- General provisions for bad debts, e.g. by applying a percentage, but reasonable provisions against specific debtors and actual bad debts are allowed.
- Entertainment expenses and gifts. Relief for entertainment of foreign customers was abolished in 1988/89. However, the general rule is relaxed for gifts to employees and gifts to any one person in a year costing no more than £50 with a conspicuous advertisement and which are not food, drink, tobacco or gift vouchers.
- Cost of appealing against income tax assessments; and accountants' fees in connection with an Inland Revenue investigation, unless there is no alteration to the Tax Return under enquiry, in which case most, if not all, the accountants' fees are allowable.
- Penalties for breaches of the law.
- Deductions for self-cancelling annuities representing tax avoidance schemes are not allowable (*Moodie v IRC 1993, HL* following *W. T. Ramsey v CIR 1982, AC*).

Allowable expenses

In general, business expenses which do not fall under the foregoing prohibitions are allowable for tax purposes but the following allowable expenses are worthy of special mention:

- Repairs and maintenance of trade premises, plant, fittings, vehicles, etc., not being of the nature of additions or improvements. Renewals are not allowed if capital allowances are claimed.
- Rent and rates of trade or professional premises. Where part of a private residence is exclusively used for the business a proportion of the rent and a proportion of any premium may be claimed. This proportion may be based on floor area.
- Employees' remuneration, directors' fees, employer's National Insurance contributions and contributions to approved superannuation funds payable

by the business. The self-employed cannot charge their own National Insurance contributions against their profits.

- Business insurance premiums, but sums received under claims must be brought into account as well as the expense.
- Travelling expenses wholly and exclusively incurred for the purpose of the business, but note that employees earning more than £8,500 and directors may have to justify reimbursed expenses and expense allowances. Travelling expenses include reasonable hotel expenses necessarily incurred.
- Losses from theft, but note that insurance receipts must also be taken into account.
- Advertising, if not of a capital nature.
- Dilapidations payable on terminations of leases to the extent that the payment represents deferred repairs.
- Losses on exchange as they accrue if clearly a risk of the trade. Consideration will be given to allowing, or treating as income, exchange differences on monetary assets and, since 6 April 1993, these differences are not subject to capital gains tax.
- Compensation to employees arising out of their terms of service; also voluntary pensions and gratuities on retirement. Redundancy payments and additions thereto up to three times the amount of the redundancy payment.
- Bank interest payable by limited companies, provided it is a proper business expense. Interest paid by the self-employed may have to be apportioned between business and private use.
- The incidental costs of obtaining loans or issuing loan stock.
- Pre-trading expenditure for trades, professions, etc. Since 1 April 1993, businesses commencing trading may claim relief for expenditure incurred in the previous seven years.
- Salaries of staff lent to charities and approved educational establishments.
- Discount and incidental costs of issuing bills of exchange accepted by banks.
- Employees' expenses on approved retraining courses, including sandwich courses, within the UK and for up to a year. The expenses include lodging, subsistence, books and travelling. The employee must have two years' service with the employer; the facility must be available to all employees of a similar class; and the course must start during employment or two years thereafter.
- Gifts of equipment to schools and other educational establishments, and other charitable gifts.
- The cost of setting up employee share incentive/option schemes.
- Accountancy expenses in preparing accounts and negotiating routine tax liabilities, but not those for Inland Revenue investigations which reveal that profits have not been fully declared.

- Cost of food and a proportion of business accommodation when working away from home (*Prior v Saunders 1993*).

Assessable income

Fewer problems arise with regard to the income side of the profit and loss account of a business. The major part of business income in the form of sales to customers or fees charged to clients needs no adjustment for tax purposes. The following, however, merit particular mention:

- Capital profits on the sale of fixed assets will affect capital allowances and may be subject to the capital gains tax provisions, but are not otherwise taxable.
- Casual profits are normally assessable either as trading income or other income.
- Exchange profits will be assessable if arising out of the trade carried on.
- Profits from illegal trading are assessable.
- Rent receivable from unfurnished letting is normally assessable as it accrues.
- Grants received are normally assessable, except where the grant is for capital expenditure or compensation for loss of capital assets.

Income not assessable

Some part of the income shown in the accounts of businesses may not be assessable for income tax or corporation tax. This will usually be the case where the income is not derived from the trade carried on or where it is of a capital nature. In the case of income not derived from the trade under assessment it is, however, possible that the Inspector of Taxes may take the view that a new trade has been established and make an assessment on those grounds. Where income is of a capital nature – for example, a profit on the sale of plant – that profit may be subject to the capital gains provisions if the proceeds exceed the original cost of the plant. Other examples of non-assessable income are as follows:

- Gifts received are not normally assessable, unless they consist of benefits to directors and higher-paid employees, and exceed £100 in a year.
- Damages receivable in a legal action are of a capital nature, and so is compensation, e.g. on cancellation of an agreement.
- Regional development grants.

PAYE and National Savings contributions

The amounts deducted from the remuneration of employees, including national insurance, are normally refunded to the Inland Revenue monthly. The payments, including National Insurance, can be made quarterly if they average less than £1,500 per month.

4.3   A SPECIMEN COMPUTATION

The following specimen computation of a fictitious business is intended to illustrate a selection of the points mentioned above. For simplicity the accounts of a partnership business are used as certain special considerations which are dealt with later apply to limited companies. Essentially, however, the method is the same whatever the form of the business concerned.

A and B in partnership
TRADING AND PROFIT AND LOSS ACCOUNT
for the year ended 31 December 2013

	£	£	£
Sales, less returns and VAT			200,000
Less: cost of goods sold			120,000
Gross Profit			**80,000**
Less: operating expenses			
Salaries:			
Partners	20,000		
Staff	18,000		
Total salaries		38,000	
National Insurance:			
Partners	2,200		
Staff	1,800		
Total National Insurance		4,000	
Premises:			
Rent and rates	2,000		
Maintenance and improvement	1,000		
Total premises expense		3,000	
Insurance:			
General	700		
Partners' life insurance	300		
Total insurance		1,000	

Travelling:			
Fares	300		
Subsistence	200		
Car expenses, inc fuel & depreciation	2,500		
Total travelling		3,000	
Entertainment		200	
Stationery & postage		400	
Advertising		800	
Donations & subscriptions:			
Local hospital	50		
Golf club	150		
Total donations		200	
Bad debts written off		300	
Provision for doubtful debts @ 5% of drs		1,200	
Depreciation of equipment		1,900	
Total operating expenses			54,000
Operating profit			**26,000**
Add: Non-trading income			
Insurance commission	150		
Profit on sale of van	350		
Total non-trading income			500
			26,500
Less: Non-trading expenses:			
Interest on loan, gross	1,420		
Interest on partners' capital	580		
Total non-trading expenses			2,000
Profit before tax			**24,500**
Less: Income tax provision			6,500
Net profit after tax			**18,000**

TAX COMPUTATION BASED ON THE ABOVE ACCOUNTS

	£	£	*Comments*
Profit before tax		24,500	*Income tax is an appropriation of profit*
Add back charges disallowed:			
Partners' salaries	20,000		*Regarded as appropriation of profit; directors' salaries would normally be allowed if the business was a limited company.*
Partners' National Insurance	2,200		
Improvements to premises	500		*A capital expense*
Car expenses	130		*Disallowed for private use – see text for details of method*
Partners' life assurance	300		*A personal expense*
Entertainment	200		*Disallowable expenses*
Golfclub subscription	150		*Probably not wholly and necessarily expended for business purposes; the amount for the local hospital may be allowed.*
Provision for doubtful debts	1,200		*Only the write-off against specific debts is allowable.*
Depreciation	1,900		*Capital allowances are available instead.*
Interest on loan	1,420		*Possibly subject to deduction of tax at source.*
Interest on partners' capital	580		*An appropriation of profit.*
		28,580	
		53,080	
Deduct income not chargeable:			
Profit on sale of van		350	*Capital – will affect capital allowances*
Adjusted profit		52,730	

The adjusted profit would be reduced by capital allowances and loss relief to arrive at taxable profits, and would be apportioned to the partners in their profit-sharing ratios. The amount so apportioned would then form part of each partner's personal computation.

Rounding of business computations

Subject to some qualifications, the Inland Revenue are prepared to accept business computations of profits rounded to the nearest £1,000. This applies where such rounding is applied to the business accounts and turnover is not less than £5 million. In particular rounding does not apply to: chargeable gains (except for incidental costs of acquisition and disposal); tax credit relief for overseas companies; accrued income and most computations of capital allowances.

4.4   CAPITAL ALLOWANCES

Meaning and purpose of 'capital allowances'

The figure for the depreciation of fixed assets which is charged in the accounts of a business is not allowable for tax purposes. Instead of depreciation, various 'capital allowances' may be deducted from the assessed profits. Many people are confused as to why depreciation is not allowed but capital allowances are. The depreciation figure in the accounts is an accounting adjustment calculated to progressively write off the assets over their useful lives (producing a 'fair and reasonable' representation of the actual value of the Company's assets). Capital allowances represent the amount of write-off which is allowed for tax purposes – normally greater than the depreciation amount for the first few years, particularly in the first year. The (faster) rate at which an asset can be written down for tax purposes bears no relation to the actual value or life of the assets concerned; it is a governmental concession designed to stimulate capital investment by offering the carrot of higher tax relief in the year of purchase. In effect the tax reliefs are all skewed towards the front end of the asset life, so that instead of having an even progression of tax reliefs, they are mostly taken in the early years, resulting in lower tax in those earlier years and correspondingly higher tax in later years. For the purpose of the accounts, the assets are recorded at their fair value, not their artificially low 'tax-written-down' value, and the amount of tax initially saved (or, in effect, deferred) as a result of the accelerated write-down may be recorded in the accounts as 'deferred tax'.

Capital allowances apply to industrial buildings, ships, mines, oil wells, plant and machinery. The term 'plant and machinery' covers a wide range and includes vehicles, furniture, fixtures and fittings for business purposes.

Capital allowances are applicable only to plant and machinery belonging to the trader, but the payment of a deposit indicates ownership. If the expenditure becomes abortive, disposal value will apply.

The *Finance Act 2008* introduced major changes in the capital allowances regime which took effect from 1 April 2008 (Corporation Tax) or 6 April 2008 (Income Tax).

The main changes can be summarised as follows:

- A new annual investment allowance (AIA) was introduced for the first £50,000 of expenditure on most plant and machinery each year. The annual investment allowance was increased to £100,000 for expenditure after 6 April 2010, but in the March 2011 Budget it was announced that the AIA was to be reduced from £100,000 to £25,000 with effect from 1 April 2012 for businesses chargeable to corporation tax and 6 April 2012 for businesses chargeable to income tax. However, AIA has become something of a political football in recent years and further changes were announced in the Autumn Statement 2012. A threshold of £250,000was announced for 1 January 2013 to 31 December 2014. However, further changes announced in the 2014 Budget mean that the £250,000 limit now applies up to 5 April 2014. A new limit of £500,000 has been introduced for the period 6 April 2014 to 31 December 2015. As things currently stand the threshold is due to revert back to £25,000 from 1 January 2016 and not 1 January 2015 as originally announced.
- Where the balance of unrelieved expenditure in the main pool is less than £1,000, a business is allowed to claim a writing down allowance sufficient to write-off the remaining balance in the pool.
- First year allowances for expenditure on business cars with CO_2 emissions of less than 110g/km were available at 100 per cent until 31 March 2013. In 2013/14 and 2014/15 the 100 per cent first year allowance is only available in relation to the purchase of new and unused (not second hand) cars with CO_2 emissions of less than 95g/km.
- A new class of assets was introduced called 'integral features' covering expenditure on such items as electrical systems, cold water systems, powered ventilation systems, lifts and escalators. Expenditure on these items can be included in the AIA but any such expenditure that does not form part of the AIA must be excluded from the main capital allowances pool and placed in a separate special rate pool to be written down at 10% per annum.
- The rate of writing down allowance on plant and machinery included in the main pool was 20%. This has been further reduced to 18% in respect of expenditure incurred on or after 1 April 2012 by companies, or 6 April 2012 by individuals.
- The rate of writing down allowance on long life assets (those with an economic life of 25 years or more) was increased from 6% to 10%.

Any expenditure on such assets after 1 April 2008 for companies, or 6 April 2008 for individuals is allocated to a 'special rate pool'. The rate of allowances on expenditure included in special rate pools was reduced to 8% for chargeable periods beginning on or after 1 April 2012 for companies or 6 April 2012 for individuals.

- A phased withdrawal of industrial buildings allowances, agricultural buildings allowances and hotel allowances over a four year period was announced so that such allowances are no longer available after 1 April 2011.
- It was originally announced that Enterprise Zone Allowances would be withdrawn from April 2011. However, the *Finance Act 2012* included provisions which effectively, re-introduces them. 100% first year allowances will be available in respect of expenditure incurred by trading companies on qualifying plant and machinery used in certain designated areas within enterprise zones. The new provisions originally allowed for the 100% allowances to be claimed in relation to expenditure incurred between 1 April 2012 and 31 March 2017. This period has since been extended to 31 March 2020.

As from 5 April 2008 there are essentially five groups of capital allowances: annual investment allowances, first-year allowances, initial allowances, writing-down allowances (formerly known as 'annual allowances' or 'wear and tear allowances') and balancing allowances or balancing charges.

Annual investment allowances (AIA)

The introduction of AIA coincides with the withdrawal of most first year allowances. It does, however, provide immediate full tax relief for businesses of all sizes not just small and medium sized businesses as was the case with first year allowances. The maximum allowance of £500,000 between 1 April 2014 and 31 December 2015 is increased or reduced in proportion to the length of the chargeable period where this is shorter or longer than one year. Where more than £500,000 is spent in a chargeable period, the excess will qualify for writing down allowances.

Businesses are permitted to claim AIA in respect of expenditure on long-life assets and integral features as well as on general plant and machinery.

The AIA complements and does not replace any of the existing 100% first year allowance schemes. Moreover, Research and Development Allowances and Business Premises Renovation Allowances are unaffected by the introduction of AIA.

Unlike first year allowances, the AIA is available in respect of expenditure on assets for leasing.

First-year allowances (FYA)

FYAs of 100% can be claimed in respect of the following types of expenditure irrespective of the size of the business:

- Certain energy-saving plant and equipment
- Cars with low CO_2 emissions
- Plant or machinery for use in gas refuelling stations prior to 31 March 2015
- Environmentally beneficial plant and machinery
- Certain new investment by companies in new plant and machinery for use in assisted areas in Enterprise Zones
- New and unused zero emissions goods vehicles in the 5 years from 1 April 2010 (corporation tax) and 6 April 2010 (income tax)

There are exclusions both general and specific exclusions on the types of expenditure for which FYAs can be claimed.

General exclusions apply in respect of the following types of expenditure:

- Cars (except those with very low carbon dioxide emissions)
- Plant or machinery for leasing
- Assets acquired initially for non-trading purposes
- Assets acquired by way of gift
- Expenditure incurred in the final period of trading.
- Plant and machinery that was initially acquired for purposes other than those of the qualifying activity

Some of the more important specific exclusions include:

- Expenditure on plant and machinery which generates electricity or heat attracting tariff payments under the Feed-in Tariff or Renewable Heat Incentive schemes.
- Certain railway assets
- Certain ships

Initial allowances

Initial allowances were special allowances that applied to expenditure on industrial and commercial buildings, including shops and offices, in Enterprise Zones. The allowance was 100% of cost including VAT unless a writing-down allowance of 25% on cost was claimed instead.

Initial allowances were withdrawn from April 2011.

Writing-down allowances

(a) Plant and machinery. Up to 1 April 2008 (Corporation Tax) and 6 April 2008 (Income Tax) the standard writing-down allowance on plant and machinery was 25%. The rate was reduced from 20% to 18% for expenditure incurred after April 2012. Certain expenditure is allocated to a 'special rate pool' for which writing down allowances are given at 8% (10% from April 2008 to April 2012). 'Special rate expenditure' refers to expenditure on thermal insulation, integral features, cars with CO_2 emissions exceeding 130g/km (160 g/km up to 2012/13) or long life assets after 1 April 2008.

Expenditure between 26 November 1996 and 1 April 2008 (Corporation Tax) and 6 April 2008 (Income Tax) on assets with a working life of at least 25 years ('long-life' assets) qualified for a writing-down allowance of 6% per annum on a reducing balance basis where the total expenditure on such assets exceeded £100,000 in any tax year. The 6% rate of writing down allowance was increased to 10% from 1 April 2008 (corporation tax) or 6 April 2008 (income tax). Any balance of unrelieved expenditure in the long-life asset pool and any new expenditure on such assets after that date is now to be allocated to a 'special rate pool'. The rate of allowance was reduced to 8% with effect from April 2012.

The writing-down allowance is an annual allowance calculated on the balance of a 'pool' of the cost or written-down values of all applicable assets.

Prior to April 2008 there was a pool for plant and machinery generally and business cars (used for business only) costing less than £12,000. A balance brought forward on the existing pool was added to the main pool. Cars with any element of private use had to be treated separately as referred to below. The maximum writing-down allowance on individual cars costing over £12,000 was £3,000 p.a. The balance in the pool was increased by the cost of assets purchased (and not included within an AIA claim) and decreased by the proceeds from any assets sold as well as by the writing-down allowance for each year.

A new capital allowances regime for cars was introduced in the Finance Act 2009. The principal change was that the concept of the "expensive car" (i.e. one costing over £12,000) disappeared. Instead, capital allowances are now given by reference to the CO_2 emissions of the car. New expenditure after 1 April 2013 (companies) and 6 April (individuals) on cars with CO_2 emissions of up to 95 gm/km will give rise to an entitlement to a 100% first year allowance. Cars used exclusively for business purposes with CO_2 emissions between 96 gm/km and 130 gm/km will be placed in the general plant and machinery pool and attract 20% writing down allowance. Cars used exclusively for business purposes with CO_2 emissions above 130 gm/km will be placed in the 8% special rate pool. There is no distinction between diesel and petrol cars when considering emissions. Cars where there is an element of private use will continue to be de-pooled as previously, but the writing down allowance will now be based on their CO_2 emissions.

If the total AIA-qualifying expenditure exceeds the £500,000 limit referred to above, an additional pool will be required in respect of expenditure on integrated features not included with an AIA claim.

From 1 April 2008 (Corporation Tax) and 6 April 2008 (Income Tax) where unrelieved expenditure in the main pool is £1,000 or less, businesses can claim to write off the remaining balance in the pool as a writing down allowance. This is intended to accelerate the claiming of writing down allowances on relatively small residual amounts left in a company's main plant and machinery pool.

Example

	AIA £	Pool £	Claim £
WDA b/fwd		30,000	
Additions qualifying for AIA	2,000		
AIA (100%)	(2,000)		2,000
Sale proceeds		(2,000)	
		28,000	
WDA 18%		(5,040)	5,040
WDA C/fwd		22,960	
Total capital allowance claimed in year			7,040

Where assets are fully written off by the 100% Annual Investment Allowance they are obviously not eligible for any writing-down allowance in addition. For assets not subject to the first-year allowance the writing-down allowance can be claimed in the year of purchase. In all instances, these allowances are the maximum claimable. The taxpayer can 'disclaim' or reduce the amount claimed, if a full claim would not attract any tax relief due to the taxable income falling below the personal allowance.

Example (using the capital allowance example above)

	£
Profits (as adjusted for tax purposes)	14,000
Less capital allowance (2,000 + 3,240)	7,040
Statutory Total income	6,960
Less personal allowance	10,000
'Wasted' capital allowance	(3,040)

The taxpayer could disclaim £3,040 of the above writing down allowances. It is often tax-efficient to claim first year allowances when available and disclaim the writing down allowance. The higher first year allowances are by their nature only available in the first year.

Amending the above allowance computation:

	AIA £	Pool £	Claim £
WDA b/fwd		30,000	
Additions qualifying for AIA	2,000		
AIA (100%)	(2,000)		2,000
Sale proceeds		(2,000)	
		28,000	
WDA (restricted)		(2,000)	2,000
WDA C/fwd		26,000	
Total capital allowance claimed in year			4,000

	£
Adjusted profits	14,000
Less capital allowance	4,000
Statutory Total income	10,000
Less personal allowance	10,000
'Wasted' capital allowance	Nil

(b) Industrial buildings, agricultural buildings and hotels. These allowances were phased out over four years starting in 2008/09. Prior to April 2008 a writing-down allowance of 4% was applied each year to the cost, including the first year, and was deducted from the written-down balance as well as the first-year allowance, where applicable.

The rate of writing-down allowance for agricultural buildings was also 4% from 1 April 1986. The 4% allowance was reduced by 1% each year starting in 2008/09 reducing to zero in 2011/12.

From 11 May 2001, 100% capital allowances are available for property owners or occupiers to claim 'up-front' tax relief on providing flats for rent. This is for expenditure on the renovation or conversion of vacant or underused space above shops or commercial premises built before 1980 in traditional shopping areas. These allowances are not affected by the withdrawal of industrial buildings, agricultural buildings and hotel allowances. These were withdrawn for expenditure after 31 March 2013(corporation tax) and 5 April 2013 (income tax).

(c) **Private cars used for business.** Expenditure on such cars is affected by the new capital allowances regime for cars introduced in the Finance Act 2009. Prior to April 2009 they had to be accounted for individually (not in a pool), and a writing-down allowance of 20% (25% prior to April 2008) was allowable on each vehicle, each year. As from April 2009 they continue to be de-pooled, but the entitlement to capital allowances depends on the CO_2 emissions of the car (see page 80). The amount of the allowance which is set off against tax will depend on the proportion of business/private use. From 2013/14 for a new car emitting up to 95 g/km, or electrically propelled, 100% first-year allowances are available.

(d) **Fixtures.** The rules which apply in respect of the claiming of plant and machinery allowances on fixtures are complex. Subject to the points made below a lessor (the person who lets the property) can claim allowances on expenditure incurred on fixtures and fittings. However, if a business tenant incurs the expenditure and the fixtures subsequently become the lessor's by operation of law, the tenant can nevertheless claim allowances. Allowances claimed cannot exceed the original cost of the fixtures when new. Vendors and purchasers may make a joint election (within 2 years of the date of the contract) fixing how much of the purchase price paid by the purchaser relates to the fixtures. The *Finance Act 2012* introduced provisions to make the availability of capital allowances to the purchaser conditional on the previous business expenditure on qualifying fixtures being pooled before the transfer to the purchaser. The seller and purchaser must also use one of two existing procedures to fix their agreement as to the transfer value of the fixtures (i.e. either by way of a joint election under the *Capital Allowances Act 2001* or through determination by a first tier tribunal). Exceptionally, a past owner may be required to provide a written statement of the amount of the disposal value of the fixtures which he had previously been required to bring into account.

Balancing allowances and balancing charges

These allowances or charges apply in the year when the asset is sold or scrapped and their purpose is to ensure that no more nor less than the net cost of an asset, after deducting receipts from the eventual sale, is allowable as a charge against taxable profits. Where the pool system is in use the sale proceeds are deducted from the balance in the pool. If the sale proceeds are greater than the pool balance, the difference is a balancing charge, i.e. added to profit. If the sale proceeds exceed the cost, then a capital gain may arise on that excess. With the pool system balancing allowances normally arise only on cessation of a business but they may arise for 'depooled' short life assets.

In addition items which have their own pool such as assets with a proportion of private use will certainly lead to a balancing adjustment, unless disposed at written-down value.

Basis period

Capital allowances refer to the accounting year on which the assessment is based. The profits of a business in single ownership or a partnership would, for the accounts year to, say, 31 December 2012, normally be assessed for the tax year 2012/13. Capital allowances to be deducted from the assessment would refer to assets acquired in the year to 31 December 2012. But see also under section 4.6 below.

Replaced plant

Where a balancing charge arises on the disposal of an asset which is to be replaced, the taxpayer can elect to deduct the balancing charge from the cost of the new asset, but this would reduce allowances on the latter.

Plant or machinery for leasing

Where plant and machinery is acquired on a finance lease lasting over 5 years, a lessee can claim Annual Investment Allowance for expenditure on plant and machinery for leasing or letting on hire. Prior to 1 April 2006, only the lessor could claim the capital allowances.

Income tax losses due to capital allowances and arising from leasing are not available for set-off against non-leasing income by individuals or partnerships, except a full-time leasing business carried on for at least six months.

Leased cars

The new capital allowances regime for cars commencing from April 2009 also changed the way in which car lease rentals are relieved. Prior to April 2009, taxis, private hire cars and those hired out for short terms, or to disabled persons, qualified for writing-down allowances of 20% (25% prior to April 2008) in the year of acquisition, with a limit to the cost of £12,000. Short term means hiring for no more than 30 days to a particular person, and for less than 90 days in 12 months.

The lessee could charge the whole cost of the rental for the car (assuming it is used for business purposes) provided the retail price was no more that £12,000. Where the retail price exceeded £12,000 the allowable charge in the lessee's computation was that proportion of the rental which is represented by the following fraction: £12,000 plus half the excess price over £12,000 divided by the price. For example, if the retail price is £20,000, the allowable proportion of the rental was:

$$\frac{12,000 + ((20,000 - 12,000)/2)}{20,000} = \frac{12,000 + 4,000}{20,000} = 80\%$$

For leases commencing after 1 April 2009 (companies) or 6 April 2009 (individuals) the car value restriction for these purposes has been abolished for all cars with CO_2 emissions up to 130gm/km (160g/km up to April 2013) thus permitting a 100% allowance of the leasing payments against the profits of businesses leasing such cars.

For cars with CO_2 emissions above 130 gm/km (160 gm/km prior to April 2013) there is a fixed percentage disallowance of 15% of the leasing payments. The restriction will not normally apply to short leases i.e. leases of 45 consecutive days or less.

Hire purchase

The business which obtains plant by means of hire purchase may claim capital allowances on all capital expenditure (excluding the interest charge) incurred under the contract as though it had been incurred when the contract began.

Security assets

From 5 April 1989, expenditure by individuals or partnerships on business security assets are eligible for capital allowances. These are assets provided to meet a special threat to an individual's security, but exclude cars, ships, aircraft and living accommodation.

Films, discs and tapes

There are special tax rules relating to companies that produce films (including television and video productions). Such rules determine how to calculate the taxable profits of film-making companies and how any tax losses may be relieved. Further information may be found on HMRC's website at www.hmrc.gov.uk/films.

Energy efficient plant and machinery

100% first year allowances are also available for expenditure in accounting periods ending on or after 6 April 2001 on new plant and machinery within stipulated categories such as heat and power systems, light and refrigeration that has been certified as meeting certain energy efficiency criteria.

Enhanced Capital Allowances

Expenditure incurred by businesses on or after 1 April 2003 on specified plant or machinery which meets strict water saving or efficiency criteria will qualify for 100% first-year allowances. Details of the qualifying plant and machinery are to be made available on the internet at www.eca.gov.uk.

4.5 TURNOVER UNDER £81,000

For many years the Inland Revenue has accepted simplified (3-line) accounts where the turnover is less than £81,000 (previously £79,000) . This information is entered on the Self-Assessment tax return. The Accounts themselves need not be submitted as well.

The arrangement applies to individuals and partnerships, including those receiving rental income below the limit. These simplified accounts are limited to a statement of turnover less the total of the business expenses arrived at in accordance with the tax rules indicated above. Details of capital allowances claimed must also be stated on the return and included in the expenses figure. The Tax Inspector may, however, call for further information, possibly full accounts, especially if a loss is shown or the business is subdivided so that each unit falls below the turnover limit. For these reasons, as well as for internal management purposes, it is always desirable for a small venture to have full accounts prepared and available.

Largely in order to expedite the processing of claims of self-employed persons claiming universal credit (the replacement for tax credits) due to be implemented from October 2013 onwards, the Government has introduced a cash basis system of accounting. The main aspects of the rules are as follows:

- It is optional for unincorporated businesses with a turnover of less than £81,000, with an entitlement to continue until annual turnover exceeds £162,000.
- It is available from 2013/14 and an election can be made by ticking a box the taxpayer's self-assessment tax return.
- In essence, income is charged to tax when received and expenses are deductible in the period in which they are paid. This means by implication that tax is not paid on bad debts because the amount receivable from the debtor is not brought into account as part of income.
- The system offers a simplified basis for expenses claims for motor expenses and use of home as an office.
- Expenditure on fixed assets (if allowable) is allowable when paid and not spread over the life of the asset.
- Buying something on hire purchase is simpler in so far as if the expense is allowable, there is no need to apportion between the interest and capital elements of the regular repayments.

- Interest on cash borrowings is only allowed up to a maximum of £500.
- There is a restriction that losses can only be carried forward against future trading profits. They cannot be offset against other income for the year or against the previous year's profits.

The decision as to whether or not to opt for the cash based system of may not be straightforward. There are advantages and disadvantages which require careful consideration. In cases of doubt it may be necessary to seek professional advice.

4.6   UNINCORPORATED BUSINESSES/PARTNERSHIPS

Basis of assessment

Assessment is made on a 'current year basis', based on profits in the accounting year ending in the tax year of assessment.

Returns of partnership income are made by a 'representative partner' and assessed on the partnership. Individual partners are required to self-assess their total income, including that from the partnership.

Cessation

Certain trading expenses are eligible for tax relief after a business ceases and can be set off against the income and/or capital gains of the individual who pays such expenses. The expenditure concerned could include that which was closely related to the former business or professional activities such as: the cost of remedying defective work, insurance premiums and legal costs in connection with defective work, debts which have become bad debts after the cessation of the business and the costs of debt collection. No relief will be given where these expenses have been charged (e.g. by way of provisions) on the business accounts. The expenditure must be incurred within 7 years after the trade ceases and claims must be made within 2 years after the year of assessment in which the expense is paid.

Change of Partners

Where one or more members of a partnership leave the firm, and where new partners are introduced, the old partnership is theoretically discontinued and a new partnership is assumed to be set up. If at least one of the old partners remains, an election can be made for tax purposes within two years of the change to treat the firm as a continuing business.

Stock valuation on cessation

The valuation of stock when a business is sold or discontinued and transferred to a connected person must be as for an arm's-length transaction.

4.7   RELIEF FOR LOSSES

Basically, there are three ways of dealing with a business loss (which means a taxable loss after adjusting the accounts in the manner set out above).

Carry forward

The first method, which applies to both unincorporated businesses and to limited companies, is to carry forward the loss and set it off against the next available profits from the same trade. If the next trading profits are insufficient to absorb the whole of the loss then the balance is carried forward to be set off against the following assessment and so on. There is no time limit except for 'hobby farmers', where the limit is six years. Capital allowances which cannot be deducted from an assessment because a loss has been incurred may also be carried forward indefinitely until they can be set off against profits. In effect, therefore, capital allowances increase the loss.

Carry-back of losses in the first three years of trading

A second method is to 'carry back' the losses. For an unincorporated business or partnership, where a loss occurred in any of the first three years of trading, that loss can be set off against profits or an individual's general income of the preceding three years, absorbing income of the earliest year first. For an incorporated business (i.e. a limited company) business losses can be carried back for one year and set off against the company's earlier profits.

A temporary extension of loss relief was announced in the 2009 budget to help businesses survive the economic recession. For losses arising in 2008/09 and 2009/10, businesses could carry back their trading losses for 3 years against profits of the same trade on a 'last in first out' (LIFO) basis. There was no restriction on the amount of the loss carry-back for one year, but loss carry-backs to the earlier two years were restricted to a maximum of £50,000 for each tax year.

Set-off against total income

A third method of dealing with a business loss, which applies only to individuals and unincorporated businesses or partnerships, is to offset the loss incurred by an individual in business against the total statutory income for the year of assessment in which the loss was incurred or the preceding year. If the total non-business taxable income of a taxpayer for 2013/14 was £15,000 and he or she sustained a loss in the business of £3,700 for the financial year to 31 March 2014, the taxpayer could claim to have the £3,700 set off against the £15,000 and thus reduce the 2013/14 assessment to £11,300 or alternatively, against total statutory income of the preceding year. A claim will be admitted only where the business which sustains the loss is carried on with a reasonable expectation of profit. The *Finance Act 2013* contains provisions which limit income tax reliefs claimed by individuals with effect from 6 April 2013 to the greater of £50,000 or 25% of income. These provisions do not apply to deductions for trade or property loss relief or post-cessation trade or property relief made from profits of the same trade or property business. They do, however, affect an individual's ability to offset trading losses or property losses against general income. For the purpose of applying these rules an individual's income is adjusted to take account of charitable donations and pension contributions.

Capital gains

Where trading losses are set off against statutory total income of a given year and there still remain excess losses, S71 ITA 2007 permits a taxpayer to offset such excess losses against capital gains for the year after deducting current year or brought forward capital losses. In such cases, the taxpayer cannot specify the amount of the claim and so the annual exempt amount may be fully or partly wasted.

4.8   COMPANIES AND CORPORATION TAX

Limited company

Limited companies and other corporate bodies are assessed for corporation tax on the profits, adjusted for tax purposes, made in the company's accounting year.

Scope and nature of the tax

Limited companies as well as most other corporate bodies and some trading clubs and unincorporated associations are liable to pay corporation tax, but not income tax, on their profits as adjusted for tax purposes. Unincorporated businesses, owned by individuals or partnerships, are assessed for income tax. Dividends paid by companies do not reduce the profit assessable to corporation tax.

Advance Corporation Tax ceased to apply from 6 April 1999. Companies are required to pay all the Corporation Tax due within nine months of their year end.

Rates of tax

The rates of corporation tax are:

(a) for **small profits companies** – small profits companies are those with profits (including dividends received plus the tax credit) up to £300,000.

Profits £		**2014/15**	**2013/14**
0-300,000	Small profits rate	20%	20%
300,001-1,500,000	Marginal rate	21.25%	23.75%
1,500,001 or more	Main rate	21%	23%
Standard fraction		1/400	3/400

Where a company has one or more associated companies, the limits were divided by the number of companies involved. A company is associated where one company controls another, or companies are under common control. For the purpose of determining whether a person has control of both companies, HMRC ignore the rights and powers of a person's relatives, unless there is substantial commercial interdependence between the two companies. Examples of commercial interdependence would include cases where one company is financially dependent on the other, where they have common customers, or where they share resources such as premises, employees or equipment.

(b) for **large companies**, 21% with effect from 1 April 2014 (previously 23%).

Where profits are above the small profits limit of £300,000 and up to £1,500,000, marginal relief applies. The marginal relief consists of the main rate of Corporation Tax on the profits, less 1/400 of the amount by which the profits fall short of the upper limit. Thus, if in 2014/15, profits were £500,000, the corporation tax would be:

	£
21% on £500,000	105,00
Less: (£1,500,000 – £500,000) x 1/400	2,500
	102,500

Alternatively this can be calculated using the marginal rate referred to above, as follows:

	£
20% on £300,000	60,000
21.25% on £200,000	42,500
	102,500

In this case the corporation tax payable of £102,500 represents an effective rate of 20.5% on the profits.

The basis of assessment

Limited companies are assessed to corporation tax on their taxable profits, less capital allowances, for each accounting period. The taxable profits include profits from all sources, including capital gains but excluding dividends received from other UK companies. Corporation tax rates are set for each year commencing on 1st April (the tax year). If an accounting period spans two tax years (i.e. it starts in one tax year and ends in another, for example starting on January 1st and ending on December 31st) the rate of corporation tax applied is the weighted average of the rates in each of the two tax years, apportioned according to the number of months of the accounting period falling in each tax year. Payment is due nine months after the end of the accounting period.

Large companies with taxable profits of £1.5 million p.a. or more moved to paying corporation tax in quarterly instalments for accounting periods ending on or after 1 July 1999. This new system was brought in over 4 years.

Computation of profit

The general rule is that a computation for corporation tax purposes is based on income tax principles and is made under the appropriate Schedules and Cases as apply to an income tax computation. The whole of the sources of income which falls under the various Schedules and Cases is, however, aggregated so that a single total is arrived at on which corporation tax is payable. The same rules as for income tax decide what income is assessable or not and what charges are allowable or not; but there are certain exceptions as explained below.

Corporation tax is chargeable on all income, however arising. Income from trading overseas is assessed whether actually received or not but overseas taxation is allowed as a deduction against such income. Dividends received from UK companies are not chargeable to corporation tax.

Capital gains (see later section) are treated as part of profits for the purpose of corporation tax and therefore chargeable at the appropriate corporation tax rate.

Yearly interest and other annual payments are deductible for corporation tax purposes and the system of capital allowances applies. Losses may be carried forward. Trading losses may be set off against other income of the same period or of preceding periods. Dividends or other forms of distribution of profit do not constitute charges against income. Under the Gift Aid Scheme, UK resident companies may obtain relief for one-off payments to charity by treating this payment as a charge against income. From April 2000, payments are made gross.

From April 2000, payments by companies under charitable covenants are relieved as Gift Aid payments, and paid gross. Prior to this date, payments under charitable covenants were relieved a as charge provided basic rate tax was deducted from the payment.

A specimen computation

The profit and loss account for a company for the year ended 31 March 2015 might show the following figures.

	£	£
Trading profit, adjusted for tax		2,770,000
Interest in government stock received 31.12.14, gross	10,000	
Dividends from UK companies, received 1.5.14, net	7,200	
		17,200
		2,787,200
Less: Debenture interest paid, on 31.12.14, gross		80,000
		2,707,200
Less: Dividends paid 1.6.14		36,600
		2,670,600

Capital gains for the year were £100,000; loss relief brought forward was £50,000; and capital allowances were £50,000. There are several associated companies, so no marginal small company relief is due.

The computation for corporation tax was as follows:

	£
Trading profit	2,770,000
Add: Interest received	10,000
	2,780,000
Less: Debenture interest	80,000
	2,700,000
Add: Capital gains	100,000
	2,800,000
Less: Capital allowances	50,000
	2,750,000

Less: Loss relief	50,000
Profits chargeable to Corporation Tax	2,700,000
Mainstream corporation tax at 21%:	567,000

Groups of companies

A loss incurred by a company which is a member of a group may be set off against the profit made by another member of the group. The test of group membership is ownership of 75% of the ordinary shares. The right to carry forward a tax loss is restricted where a change in the ownership of a company is associated with a change in the nature of its trade.

4.9   INVESTMENT COMPANIES AND CLOSE COMPANIES

General

An investment company is one whose main purpose is to make and obtain income from investments. These include companies formed for the purpose of administering family investments in securities and land; but there are many large investment companies. The taxable profits of these companies (as well as those of insurance companies) are assessed after deducting 'management expenses' (s 75 Taxes Act 1988), which are essentially the expenses of managing the company.

Excess management expenses and charges (such as interest payments) cannot be claimed where, during a three-year period, the ownership of an investment company changes, the business has become small or negligible and is revived after the change, or there is a significant increase in capital three years after the change or before the change.

Close companies

A close company is one which does not have a quotation on a stock exchange and of which less than 35% of the shares are held by the public. More specifically it is one controlled by five or fewer 'participators' and their associates, of which all partners and near relatives are treated as one individual for the purpose. Close investment companies are liable for corporation tax at 23% on profits. The small companies' rate does not apply to these companies, nor the starting rate.

A close company making a loan to a participator used to be liable to tax on the amount of the loan, within 14 days after the end of the accounting period. This provision extended to directors' overdrawn current accounts. This provision proved to be virtually impossible to operate as very few companies could establish the figures within 14 days of the year end. Accordingly, in the 1995 Budget this period was extended to 9 months for accounting periods ending on or after 31 March 1996. In addition, no tax is to be paid if the 'loan' is repaid within this 9 months. If it is repaid after this 9-month period, the tax is paid a year later.

The Government has introduced changes to the way the corporation tax charge on loans to participators operates which take effect from 20 March 2013. The aim of the changes is to:

- ensure that loans to partnerships and trusts are caught
- bring transfers of value other than loans within the scope of the charge, and
- prevent temporary repayment of loans (sometimes termed 'bed and breakfasting').

4.10　SELF-EMPLOYED PERSONS

A. Employed or self-employed?

The *Income Tax (Earnings and Pensions) Act 2003* basically applies to persons who work for wages or salaries under a contract of employment. The *Income Tax (Trading and Other Income) Act 2005* Part 2 applies to persons or partners operating a separate business. Apart from remuneration, the advantages of being employed under a contract of service include possible inclusion in the employer's pension scheme, redundancy pay, maternity pay and other business and social security benefits. On the other hand a person operating his or her own business receives more tax allowances for business expenses, but has to pay for pensions, and must, of course, provide capital and accept risk. To decide whether you are employed or self-employed for tax purposes, try the following questions.

Employed

If you can answer 'yes' to these questions, you are probably **employed**:

- Do you yourself have to do the work rather than hire someone else to do it for you?
- Can someone tell you at any time what to do or when to do it?
- Are you paid by the hour, week or month? Can you get overtime pay?
- Do you work set hours, or a given number of hours a week or month?
- Do you work at the premises of the person you work for or at a place or places he or she decides?

Self-employed

If you can answer 'yes' to these questions, it will usually mean you are **self-employed**:

- Do you have the final say in how the business is run?

- Do you risk your own money in the business?
- Are you responsible for meeting the losses as well as taking the profits?
- Do you provide the main items of equipment you need to do your job, not just the small tools many employees provide for themselves?
- Are you free to hire other people on your own terms to do the work you have taken on? Do you pay them out of your own pocket?
- Do you have to correct unsatisfactory work in your own time and at your own expense?

(For more information on this topic, see IR leaflet ES/FS1 'Employed or self-employed for tax and National Insurance contributions.)

The tax situation for various occupations is examined below.

B. Authors, artists and entertainers

Authors, artists and entertainers, conducting a business on their own account and not employed at a salary, are assessed as income from trade. This means that they can charge against their income the expenses wholly and exclusively incurred in earning that income. The expenses would include: stationery, postage, materials used in the activity, the wardrobe of an actor, and the costs of a study or studio, such as heating, cleaning, rates and rent. If the work is done at home, a proportion of the actual outgoings associated with the accommodation may be charged. Income from royalties or from an outright sale of the work is assessable and must be included in the return, but a lump sum received on sale of the residual rights of a work can be spread forward up to six years, provided the work has been published for 10 years.

Authors and creative artists are allowed to average profits over two years if their income in any one year is less than 70% of taxable income in the previous year, with marginal relief if income is between 70% and 75% of income in the preceding year. This allows them to reduce the overall tax charge for the two years and is similar to the averaging option available to farmers (see below).

Since 1969, tax cannot be avoided by selling future earnings for a capital sum, this having become a fairly common practice in the theatrical profession.

Since 1987/88, non-resident entertainers and sportsmen have had a withholding tax at the basic rate deducted from their UK earnings of at least £500.

Where a theatrical artist works under a contract of employment, his or her remuneration is chargeable to tax as income from employment, for which the deductible expenses are very limited. However, from 1990/91 the employed entertainer can deduct from his or her remuneration the fees paid to an agent who carries on an employment agency under licence. The fees deductible are limited to 17.5% of the emoluments. These provisions apply to a person who is employed as an actor, singer, musician, dancer or theatrical artist.

C. Divers

From 1978/79 the income of divers and diving supervisors operating in the UK or the continental shelf is chargeable as income from trade, and not as income from employment.

D. Farmers

(i) General. Subject to certain special arrangements noted below, farming is assessable to tax as income from trade. Assuming the farm is not operated as a limited company, losses incurred by individual farmers can be set off against other income, provided the farm is conducted with a view to profit. No set-off against other income is available to 'hobby farmers' (i.e. those operating without the expectation of profit) and not normally if losses have been incurred after 6 years. Hobby farmers can, however, claim for losses to be carried forward to be set off against any future profits. They may also claim relief against other income for the agricultural use of a farmhouse to the extent that this expenditure cannot be set off against farming income.

(ii) Averaging profits. After 1977/78 individual farmers and partnerships of farmers (not companies) have averaged profits over two consecutive years of assessment, where there is a difference of at least 30% in the profits of these years, with marginal relief for a difference between 25% and 30%.

(iii) Grants. Grants and other government subsidies are included in taxable profits if they represent revenue, not capital receipts.

(iv) Farmhouse. Only the expenses incurred in the business use of the farmhouse is allowed in computing farm profits for tax purposes.

(v) Herd basis. The 'herd' basis of assessment means that by an election within 2 years after the first year of assessment, production herds are treated as capital expenditure, not as stock in trade. Production herds are those intended for obtaining from them product for sale, such as wool and milk, but not livestock for resale in the normal course. Rearing costs and additions, but not replacements to the herd, are also capitalised and do not enter into the tax assessment, nor does the sale of the livestock. Sale of the products of the herd is, however, taxable.

(vi) VAT. The VAT position of farmers has, historically been relatively simple in so far as outputs were generally zero rated and the farmer could claim input VAT. With farmers seeking to protect their financial security through land diversification, greater attention to the charging of VAT is required along with such matters as annual accounting, flat-rate schemes for small businesses, partial exemption and capital good schemes.

(vii) Woodlands. The taxation of income from woodlands was abolished in 1988-89. However, profit on short rotation coppice is taxed as farming. This is where fast-growing trees are regularly harvested for fuel.

E. Ministers of religion

Ministers of religion may claim a deduction from income for expenses wholly, exclusively and necessarily incurred in carrying out their duties, e.g. motor and travelling expenses so incurred, postage, stationery, the replacement of robes, out-of-pocket payments to curates and lay workers, telephone charges, communion expenses, etc. A minister who pays the rent of his or her private residence may claim a deduction for whatever proportion of that residence is used in connection with his or her duties up to a maximum of one quarter. A claim can also be made for lighting, heating, and so on, according to the proportion attributable to professional purposes. A case in 1986 decided that a vicar was not entitled to claim capital allowances for a slide projector, because he did not have to incur the expenditure for his work. However a vicar can claim capital allowance on his or her car and office furniture and equipment.

F. Barristers

Prior to April 1998 barristers and certain other self-employed professional persons were taxed on a 'cash basis' – that is, their tax computations covered only actual cash received and paid and did not include amounts due but unpaid. This practice meant that when they ceased to follow their profession, or retired, fees received in cash after cessation escaped tax.

The *Finance Act 1998* revoked this privileged treatment and required these firms to include work in progress as defined by SSAP9 in their taxable income. Where time ledgers record staff time, then a useful starting point can be using the proportion of the charge-out rate covering salaries and overhead recovery. Partners' work in progress would normally only include overhead allocation.

The first year affected by these provisions was 1999/00, and firms changing from cash accounting to the new basis were allowed to spread the additional up-front tax charge when work-in-progress was first brought into account (known as the 'catch-up charge') over 10 years. The last catch-up charge payment was accounted for in the tax return for the year to 5 April 2009.

G. Subcontractors in construction industry

Subcontractors in the construction industry are subject to a system which provides for deduction of tax at source on payments within the industry, unless the contractor holds an exemption certificate.

Before 6 April 2007 if a subcontractor held a Gross Payment Certificate

(GPC) issued by the Inland Revenue, the contractor could pay him gross. If he did not hold a GPC but did have a Registration Card, the contractor made a tax deduction from the labour element of the payment (18%) which was then be paid over to the Inland Revenue.

If a subcontractor did not have either a GPC or a Registration Card, the contractor was required to treat him as an employee and payments to the subcontractor had to be made under PAYE.

After 6 April 2007 a new scheme was introduced. Compared with the previous system the main changes are:

- registration cards (CIS4) and gross payment certificates (CIS6 and CIS5) have been replaced with a verification service;
- a new employment status declaration has been introduced; and
- the vouchers in the pre-April 2007 scheme have been replaced with periodic returns.

The deduction rates for the new scheme are 20% for subcontractors registered with HMRC for payment under deduction and 30% for those not registered.

The operational detail of the construction industry scheme from 6 April 2007 is contained in the *Income Tax (Construction Industry Scheme) Regulations 2005 (SI 2005/2045)*. The new regulations provide for the registration of subcontractors for gross or net payment, the verification of subcontractors' payment status by contractors and the making of monthly returns by contractors. They also provide for certain persons and payments to be exempted from certain provisions of the scheme.

4.11 WITHHOLDING TAX

Note that companies must withhold income tax on certain payments made to overseas suppliers. International withholding tax may be required for

- financing, i.e. dividends or interest
- the use of intellectual property, i.e. royalties and licence fees
- consultancy fees and management fees
- rental of real estate, and other payments connected with real estate

In such cases the procedure by which tax is accounted for to HM Revenue and Customs involves the completion of form CT61 on a quarterly basis.

Under an EU Directive, companies may pay royalties and interest without deducting tax where such payments are made to an associated company i.e. where one company directly owns 25% of the capital or voting rights in the other or a third company directly owns 25% of both.

5

Capital Gains

5.1 GENERAL NATURE OF THE TAX

Capital gains tax (CGT) is a tax on the increase in value of an asset from the date of acquisition until the date it is disposed of (or deemed to be disposed of). If assets are disposed of for less than acquisition cost, a capital loss arises and there are provisions within the Taxes Acts to allow such losses to be offset against chargeable gains.

Gains arising from a period of ownership before 31 March 1982 are not charged to tax.

As CGT is a tax on capital gains it follows that it is not charged on profits that are assessed to Income Tax or Corporation Tax as trading income. There is, however, some overlap. For example, gains on the sale of leases may be partly assessable to CGT and partly to Income Tax or Corporation Tax.

CGT is chargeable in respect of chargeable gains incurred by persons who were resident and ordinarily resident in the UK during the tax year in which the gain arose. Persons resident in the UK are chargeable to CGT on their worldwide gains. Thus, for example, a UK resident taxpayer who disposes of a foreign holiday home is chargeable to UK CGT on any gain arising.

The gains of husband and wife are assessed separately. Individuals do not pay tax on the first £11,000 in 2014/15 (£10,900 in 2013/14). There are many other exemptions (see below). Most trusts are exempt to half the usual rate. Full exemption will, however, apply to trusts for the mentally handicapped, persons receiving attendance allowance, and the middle or higher range of disability allowance.

Major changes to the Capital Gains Tax regime were brought in with effect from 6 April 2008.

In summary the main changes were:

- The withdrawal of indexation and taper relief.
- The introduction of a new single rate of charge to CGT at 18% for individuals, trustees and personal representatives.
- Simplification of the share identification rules. These rules seek to establish which shares are disposed of in cases where taxpayers have acquired a portfolio of the same shares over a period of time.

The *Finance Act (No 2) Act* introduced a new tax rate of 28% for all higher-rate taxpayers, starting with effect on 23 June 2010. To the extent that taxable gains when aggregated with income do not exceed the higher rate tax threshold, they are taxed at 18%. At the same time it was announced that the lifetime gains eligible for Entrepreneur's Relief would be increased from £2 million to £5 million (see below). In the 2011 Budget the lifetime limit was increased to £10 million for qualifying disposals on or after 6 April 2011.

5.2 RATES OF TAX

Limited companies

Both small and large companies bear corporation tax on their capital gains at the appropriate corporation tax rates.

Investment trusts, unit trusts and funds in court

The *Finance Act 1980* gave these bodies complete exemption from capital gains. Investors are liable for capital gains tax on the realisation of their interests in the trusts.

Individuals

Prior to 6 April 2008 individuals were liable to capital gains tax at their marginal rate of income tax. In 2007/08, gains were taxable at 10%, 20% or 40%. Most trustees and personal representatives were chargeable at the rate applicable to trusts which, for 2007/08 was 40% (for details of the exceptions see Inheritance Tax Simplified). From 6 April 2008 until 22 June 2010, the 18% rate referred to in 5.1 above applied to all individuals. From 23 June 2010, a new rate of 28% applies to all individuals paying the higher rate of tax (i.e. for 2013/14 individuals whose taxable income plus taxable gains exceed £32,010). Pre 23 June gains do not count when calculating the amount of basic rate tax band used up in 2010/11.

5.3 THE PRINCIPAL EXCEPTIONS

The following gains are not chargeable to the tax:

*   The principal residence of an individual or a house which he or she owns and occupies or which is occupied rent free by a dependent relative before 6 April 1988, or where a person is required by the terms of his employment to live in other accommodation. See below for further comment.
*   Vehicles of the private car type not used for business.

- Goods and chattels sold for no more than £6,000. For a sale price above these limits the gain is limited to 5/3rds of the excess.
- Certain forms of savings, such as: National Savings Certificates, National Development Bonds, Defence Bonds, Save As You Earn and TESSA bonuses, ISA gains and Premium Bonds.
- Sums received on the maturity or surrender of life assurance policies by the original owner, or where they are gifts to the taxpayer.
- Moveable property with predictable life of under 50 years, e.g. wasting assets, such as animals and boats, not subject to capital allowances. Special provisions apply to leases of 50 years or less. Other wasting assets must be written down progressively and only the balance of cost can be set against sale proceeds for capital gains purposes.
- The first £11,000 of capital gains in 2014/15 (£10,900 in 2013/14). Both husband and wife obtain this exemption.
- Gains on the disposal of British government securities and those guaranteed by the British government; and corporate bonds, debentures and loan stock, if the company has a quotation on a stock exchange, but not loans convertible into shares, unmarketable securities, those carrying excessive interest and those linked to a share index.
- Gifts to charities and the capital gains of charities.
- Gifts or sales by a taxpayer to his or her spouse or civil partner, but in this case the spouse/partner will be assumed to have acquired the asset at the date and cost when it was originally acquired.
- From 13 March 1989, gifts of certain business assets are available for hold over relief – see below under 'Gifts'.
- The first £5,500 of gains for trusts in 2014/15 (£5,450 in 2013/14), or £11,000 for trusts for people with learning difficulties and those receiving the middle or higher rate of disability living allowance.
- The first disposal of shares under the Enterprise Investment Scheme.
- Capital gains in personal equity plans.
- Capital gains which relate to the period before 1 April 1982.

5.4   CALCULATING THE GAIN

The general method

A capital gain or loss is essentially the difference between the cost of an asset and the proceeds of sale. The costs include the incidental expenses incurred on acquisition or disposal, e.g. professional fees, commission and stamp duty.

Prior to 6 April 2008 deductions were permitted in respect of indexation allowance and taper relief. Indexation allowance was deducted to offset inflation in the period from 31 March 1982 to 5 April 1998 in the case of individuals. It was calculated by reference to the later of 31 March 1982 or the date the asset was acquired. The legislation is complex and special rules apply to part disposals of investments, disposals and acquisitions of investments in the same period of stock exchange account, investments pooled for tax purposes, transfers between company groups and disposals in company reorganisations and reconstructions. The March 1998 budget abolished the indexation allowance (not for companies) with effect from 6 April 1998. However, for an asset held before that date an allowance for indexation was available up to 5 April 1998.

From 6 April 1998 onwards, Taper Relief was available (see below). However, for all disposals on or after 6 April 2008 both indexation allowance and taper relief are withdrawn.

CGT disclosure requirements

The Finance Bill 2003 included measures to simplify the operation of CGT. For 2003/04 tax returns and subsequent years, individuals, trustees and personal representatives do not need to complete the Capital Gains pages of the tax return provided:

- the total of their chargeable gains, after taper relief, does not exceed their annual exempt amount, and
- the total proceeds from the sale of non-exempt assets in the year does not exceed four times the annual exempt amount for individuals (previously twice the annual amount).

This rule will not apply where taxpayers wish to utilise losses to offset against gains. In this case, the Capital Gains Tax pages will need to be completed.

Indexation (from 1 April 1982)

For **corporate entities**, indexation continues to apply after 5 April 1998. The new lower rate of CGT does not apply to corporate entities which remain liable to pay Corporation Tax on their chargeable gains.

The Retail Price Index figures published are set out below.

Prices at January 1987 = 100

Year	Jan	Feb	Mar	Apr	May	Jun	Jul	Aug	Sep	Oct	Nov	Dec
1982	–	–	79.44	81.04	81.26	81.85	81.88	81.90	81.85	82.26	82.66	82.51
1983	82.61	82.97	83.12	84.28	84.64	84.84	85.30	85.68	86.06	86.36	86.67	86.89
1984	86.84	87.20	87.48	88.64	88.97	89.20	89.10	89.94	90.11	90.67	90.95	90.87
1985	91.20	91.94	92.80	94.78	95.21	95.41	95.23	95.49	95.44	95.59	95.92	96.05
1986	96.25	96.60	96.73	97.67	97.85	97.79	97.52	97.82	98.30	98.45	99.29	99.62
1987	100.0	100.4	100.6	101.8	101.9	101.9	101.8	102.1	102.4	102.9	103.4	103.3
1988	103.3	103.7	104.1	105.8	106.2	106.6	106.7	107.9	108.4	109.5	110.0	110.3
1989	111.0	111.8	112.3	114.3	115.0	115.4	115.5	115.8	116.6	117.5	118.3	118.8

Year	Jan	Feb	Mar	Apr	May	Jun	Jul	Aug	Sep	Oct	Nov	Dec
1990	119.5	120.2	121.4	125.1	126.2	126.7	126.8	128.1	129.3	130.3	130.0	129.9
1991	130.2	130.9	131.4	133.1	133.5	134.1	133.8	134.1	134.6	135.1	135.6	135.7
1992	135.6	136.3	136.7	138.8	139.3	139.3	138.8	138.9	139.4	139.9	139.7	139.2
1993	137.9	138.8	139.3	140.6	141.1	141.0	140.7	141.3	141.9	141.8	14.6	141.9
1994	141.3	142.1	142.5	144.2	144.7	144.7	144.0	144.7	145.0	145.2	145.3	146.0
1995	146.0	146.9	147.5	149.0	149.6	149.8	149.1	149.9	150.6	149.8	149.8	150.7
1996	150.2	150.9	151.5	152.6	152.9	153.0	152.4	153.1	153.8	153.8	153.9	154.4
1997	154.4	155.0	155.4	156.3	156.9	157.5	157.5	158.5	159.3	159.5	159.6	160.0
1998	159.5	160.3	160.8	162.6	163.5	163.4	163.0	163.7	164.4	164.5	164.4	164.4
1999	163.4	163.7	164.1	165.2	165.6	165.6	165.1	165.5	166.2	166.5	166.7	167.3
2000	166.6	167.5	168.4	170.1	170.7	171.1	170.5	170.5	171.7	171.6	172.1	172.2
2001	171.1	172.0	172.2	173.1	172.2	174.4	173.3	174.0	174.6	174.3	173.6	173.4
2002	173.3	173.8	174.5	175.7	176.2	176.2	175.9	176.4	177.6	177.9	178.2	178.8
2003	178.4	179.3	179.9	181.2	181.5	181.3	181.3	181.6	182.5	182.6	182.7	183.5
2004	183.1	183.8	184.6	185.7	186.5	186.8	186.8	187.4	188.1	188.6	189.0	189.9
2005	188.9	189.6	190.5	191.6	192.0	192.2	192.2	192.6	193.1	193.3	193.6	194.1
2006	193.4	194.2	195.0	196.5	197.7	198.5	198.5	199.2	200.1	200.4	201.1	202.7
2007	201.6	203.1	204.4	205.4	206.2	207.3	206.1	207.3	208.0	208.9	209.7	210.9
2008	209.8	211.4	212.1	214.0	215.0	216.8	216.5	217.2	218.4	217.7	216.0	212.9
2009	210.1	211.4	211.3	211.5	212.8	213.4	213.4	214.4	215.3	216.0	216.6	218.0
2010	217.9	219.2	220.7	222.8	223.6	224.1	223.6	224.5	225.3	225.8	226.8	228.4
2011	229.0	231.3	232.5	234.4	235.2	235.2	234.7	236.1	237.9	238.0	238.5	239.4
2012	238.0	239.9	240.8	242.5	241.8	242.8	242.1	243.0	244.2	245.6	245.6	246.8
2013	245.8	247.6	248.7	249.5	250.0	249.7	249.7	251.0	251.9	251.9	252.1	253.4
2014	252.6	254.2	254.8	255.7	255.9							

Using RI as either (1) the Retail Price Index for March 1982 if the asset was acquired prior to April 1981, or (2) the month falling 12 months after the date on which the asset was acquired or expenditure incurred if the asset was acquired from April 1981 onwards, and using RD as the Retail Price Index for the month in which the disposal was made (or April 1998 if later and an individual), the indexation allowance is calculated by the formula:

$$\frac{RD - RI}{RI} \quad \text{rounded to the nearest decimal place}$$

Corporations disposing of assets acquired before 31st March 1982 will, from 1 April 2008, be obliged to use the value at 31st March 1982 as the base cost.

5.5 ENTREPRENEURS' RELIEF

Entrepreneurs' relief arose following the storm of protest which greeted the abolition of taper relief. Taper relief was introduced from 6 April 1998 in relation to the capital gains of individuals. It reduced the chargeable gain according to the length of time an asset has been held and whether the asset has been held as a business asset or a non-business asset. It was intended to provide a tax incentive for longer term holding of assets. Entrepreneurs' relief seeks to encourage entrepreneurship by giving small entrepreneurs the prospect of paying a lower rate of tax when they come to dispose of their businesses. It works by reducing what would otherwise be chargeable gains by a percentage. It is not, however, a direct replacement for taper relief and, consequently, some people who would have qualified for taper relief will not qualify for entrepreneurs' relief (for example, employee shareholders with less than 5% holdings).

Claims need to be made on or before the first anniversary of 31 January following the tax year in which the qualifying business disposal was made.

A qualifying business disposal means a material disposal of business assets, a material disposal of trust business assets or a disposal associated with a relevant material disposal. A disposal of business assets refers to

- the disposal of the whole or part of a business
- the disposal of, or interests in, one or more assets in use for the purpose of a business when that business ceases to be carried on, or
- the disposal of, or interests in, shares or securities of a company.

The relief originally operated by reducing the amount of qualifying gains by 4/9 (or 9/14 for higher rate taxpayers) so that gains were effectively charged to CGT at 10% (as was the case with business assets taper relief). For qualifying disposals on or after 23 June 2010 relevant gains are aggregated and the resulting chargeable gain taxed at 10%, provided the gains together with previous gains subject to entrepreneur's relief do not exceed the lifetime limit. As from 1 April 2011 the relief is subject to a lifetime limit of £10 million (previously £5 million), but disposals before 6 April 2008 will not count towards the lifetime limit. Relief given to trustees will count towards the lifetime limit of qualifying beneficiaries.

Example

Mr A has, for several years, held a 25% stake in a successful family-owned company, of which he is the chairmen. He is a higher-rate tax payer. On 31 December 2013 he sells his shares to his son, making a gain of £12,000,000. Assuming his CGT annual allowance is covered by other gains, his chargeable amount is calculated as:

	£
Gain up to lifetime limit (£10,000,000) @10%	1,000,000
Balance of gain (£2,000,000) @ 28%	560,000
Total CGT payable	1,560,000

5.6   TRUSTEES

A detailed treatment of the capital gains tax position of trustees is beyond the scope of this book. The notes below merely describe the general position and any trustee readers are advised to seek professional advice in relation to trust capital gains tax matters.

Where a trust is created by will or intestacy, the trustees take the assets passing to the trust at probate value as would any other legatee under the will or intestacy. They are deemed to have acquired the assets at the date of death.

Where trusts are created during the settlor's lifetime, the settlor makes a disposal of assets to the trustees at market value. In such cases gift relief (whereby any capital gains tax due on the disposal by the settlor to the trustees is deferred) may be available, provided the trust is not 'settlor interested' i.e. the settlor could benefit from the trust property.

Where the trustees dispose of assets within the trust they are liable for capital gains tax at 28% to the extent that such gains exceed £5,500 in 2014/15 (£5,450 in 2013/14).

If a trustees distributes trust assets to a trust beneficiary this will usually be treated as a deemed disposal at market value by the trustees. In such cases gift relief as described above may be available.

The beneficiary of an overseas trust is liable to pay capital gains tax on remittances to him or her of the trust's gains. There is no exemption from the tax when an interest in an overseas trust is disposed of.

5.7   LOSSES

Losses on the sale of assets can be set off against capital gains and any losses not used in this way can be carried forward. Losses brought forward will be used only to the extent necessary to reduce gains to the exemption limit (£11,000 in 2014/15); any unutilised losses can then be carried forward to the next period.

Losses incurred by individuals on the disposal of shares taken up in unquoted trading companies may be set off against income for income tax purposes; balances unrelieved in this way can be set off against capital gains.

The allowable losses for these purposes include losses incurred from irrecoverable loans and payments under guarantees granted to borrowers for trading purposes. This relief is not applicable to loans between members of a group of companies.

5.8   REPLACEMENT OF ASSETS (ROLLOVER RELIEF)

This relief enables the payment of capital gains tax to be postponed, possibly indefinitely, when a business asset is sold and is replaced by another business asset. It applies to land and buildings, fixed plant, ships and aircraft, property let commercially and let as furnished holiday accommodation, and goodwill, and it is not necessary that the new asset is of the same kind as the old asset. It does not apply to movable plant or machinery, farming, property development, or where half a company's assets are held in land, or motor cars. The treatment varies according to whether the asset concerned is a depreciating asset or a non-depreciating asset.

In the case of the sale of a **non-depreciating business asset**, e.g. land and buildings, the capital gain is set off against the cost of the new asset – i.e. the gain is not taxable, but the base cost of the replacement asset for CGT purposes is reduced by amount of the gain, thus deferring any capital gains tax payable until the new asset is sold. However, a gain on the sale of a new asset could again be rolled over by a further replacement and so on indefinitely. Rollover relief is available to landlords selling land or buildings to tenants who have rights to acquire the freehold reversions under the *Leasehold Reform Act 1967,* the *Housing and Urban Development Act 1993* and the *Housing Acts 1985 to 1996*, provided reinvestment is made in replacement land and buildings.

Where a **depreciating business asset** is sold and replaced the capital gain is not deducted from the base cost of the replacement but is postponed for 10 years unless meanwhile the new asset has been sold (when the carried-forward gain will be deducted from the base cost of the replacement asset now sold) or replaced by a non-depreciating business asset (when the gain may be carried forward on the basis described in the previous paragraph). Depreciating assets are those with a predictable life of under 50 years such as boats and animals, and leases with an unexpired term of 60 years.

In all cases the new asset must be acquired not earlier than one year before and not later than three years after the sale of the old asset, but there can be some flexibility in these limits by agreement of the Inspector, in certain circumstances.

If the cost of a replacement asset is less than the gross proceeds from the sale of the old asset then the difference (if less than the gain) represents the capital gain on which tax must be paid and only the balance of the gain can be rolled over. If the difference is greater than the gain, no tax may be rolled over. For example, if an asset is sold for £100,000 with a chargeable gain of £50,000, and a replacement asset is then purchased for £70,000, the following occurs: a gain of £30,000 (£100,000 – £70,000) is immediately chargeable to tax; and the residual gain of £20,000 (£50,000 less the £30,000 immediately chargeable) is rolled over.

The amount of the gains which can be rolled over into a qualifying investment cannot exceed the acquisition cost of the replacement investment.

Rollover relief can be applied to EU quota premium given to producers of ewes and calves and suckler cows, milk and potatoes.

Rollover relief applies when one company in a group transfers an asset to another group member at a gain. The relief does not apply to so-called 'roll around' when assets are transferred within a group but no replacement asset is acquired. The relief does apply where land is disposed of by one member of a group as a result of compulsory purchase, and replacement land is acquired by another group member.

5.9 DEATH OF THE TAX-PAYER

No capital gains tax is usually payable but there may be a liability for inheritance tax (see Chapter 9). The persons who inherit the assets are assumed to take them at their market value at the date of death. This treatment applies to settled property on which the deceased had an interest.

Personal representatives can charge the expenses of establishing title in computing the gains or losses on the sale of assets in a deceased person's estate. Either the actual justifiable expenses can be claimed, or, if more convenient, reference can be made to the published HMRC scale of acceptable charges to determine the appropriate level of costs to be claimed in the assessment. From the same date corporate trustees must apply a further scale of charges for transfers of assets to beneficiaries and for actual disposals and acquisitions.

5.10 PAYMENT OF TAX

Payment is due on 31 January after the end of the tax year in which the gains accrued.

5.11 SALE OF PRIVATE HOUSE

As mentioned in section 5.3 above, capital gains tax is not payable on the sale of the principal private residence owned and occupied by a taxpayer. If the taxpayer owns and occupies more than one private residence he or she should advise the Inspector of Taxes which is to be treated as the principal private residence for exemption purposes. Subject to the qualifications set out below, the taxpayer will be liable for a proportion of the gain on the sale of the principal private residence corresponding to the periods when he or she was not in occupation of that house:

- Exemption is applied to a house owned by the taxpayer and occupied rent free by a dependent relative before 6 April 1988.
- Absence due to having to live elsewhere under a contract of employment is ignored, e.g. a vicar who has to live in his or her parish; so is up to four years' total absences due to working away from home; and all absences while working abroad.
- In the case of disposals before 5 April 2014, periods of absence of up to three years in total are ignored, and so are absences in the last three years for the purposes of selling the house. From 6 April 2014 the period of three years is reduced to eighteen months.
- Full exemption applies where part of a house is let as residential accommodation, provided the part let does not exceed the part occupied by the taxpayer, with a maximum relief of £40,000.
- Where a taxpayer carries on a business in part of a house exclusively set aside for that purpose, there will be a liability for capital gains tax on that part. The mere use of non-exclusive facilities, even if a charge is claimed in the business assessment, should not, however, give rise to a capital gains assessment.

5.12 SPOUSES AND CIVIL PARTNERS

With independent taxation of married women after 5 April 1990, the wife is liable for tax on the gains made from the disposal of the assets she owns. She will pay at 18% or 28% on her chargeable gains in 2014/15 and will be entitled to her own annual exemption limit of £11,000. Where assets are owned jointly by husband and wife, any gain will be shared equally, in the absence of other evidence as to the ownership of shares. By transferring investments and other chargeable assets from one party to the other full advantage can be taken of each party's exemption limits. See 5.17 Bed and Breakfasting.

The Government has introduced rules whereby civil partnerships formed as a result of the *Civil Partnerships Act 2004* are treated the same as married couples for tax purposes. From 5 December 2005, tax charges and reliefs and anti-avoidance rules apply equally to married couples and civil partners.

5.13 GIFTS

A gift from one person to another is a 'disposal' and if the market value of the asset at the time when the gift was made exceeds the cost, the difference is basically a capital gain. To the extent that an asset is transferred at a price below open market value the difference is treated as a gift. No tax is payable by the giver of a chattel when the gift is below the chattels exemption limit of £6,000. Nor would the giver be liable to capital gains tax where his total capital gains in a tax year were within the tax-free limits.

Hold-over relief

In the case of gifts of certain gifts, the capital gain implied by the gift can be carried forward and deducted from the implied base cost of the recipient of the gift. The capital gains tax liability is thus deferred until the recipient sells or otherwise disposes of the gifted asset. The assets concerned are as follows: assets of a trade, profession, vocation or family company including shares in a family trading company or in unquoted trading companies; agricultural property where the giver has vacant possession; heritage property; charitable gifts and those to political parties (with some qualifications) and housing associations; and capital paid from accumulation and maintenance trusts not later than payments of income.

Capital gains tax on gifts may be paid by ten equal annual instalments on disposals of land, unquoted shares, and controlling holdings of quoted shares, subject to an election being made. The Inland Revenue Shares Valuation Office will value unquoted shares at 31 March 1982 where all shareholders with similar holdings agree.

5.14   COMPANY LEAVING GROUP

Where a company leaves a group any asset acquired from another group member within the preceding 6 years is a deemed disposal of the asset at the date of acquisition. The chargeable gain or loss accrues immediately before the company left the group. The 1994 Budget contained measures to prevent tax avoidance by artificial degrouping.

5.15   REINVESTMENT IN EIS SHARES

Investors may defer gains made on any assets by investing in shares which, broadly, qualify for relief under the Enterprise Investment Scheme (EIS). Re-investment in EIS shares must be made within the period one year before to three years after the gain accrues.

The shares must be newly issued and fully paid. Relief is not available for shares purchased from another investor.

The amount of the gain that can be deferred is the lower of:

(i)   the amount subscribed by the investor for EIS shares, or

(ii)   the amount specified in the claim.

Note that there is no limit of £1,000,000 per annum (previously £500,000) to the amount of gains that can be deferred under this provision. The £1,000,000 limit relates to the EIS income tax relief provisions.
The deferred gain will become chargeable if:

- (a) the investor disposes of the new shares, or
- (b) the shares cease to be eligible for relief within 3 years of issue, or
- (c) the investor becomes non-resident and not ordinarily resident within 3 years of the shares being issued.

5.16   BED AND BREAKFASTING

'Bed and Breakfasting' is a stock market expression describing the practice of selling shares, then immediately repurchasing them in order to crystallise capital gains (to utilise an annual exemption) or losses (to offset other gains). Typically a sale late on day 1 is followed by a similar purchase early on day 2, when hopefully the price will be much the same.

However, following the 1998 budget, disposals and acquisitions by individuals or trustees of shares of the same class in the same company within a 30-day period are to be matched for capital gain so that no gain or loss is realised.

However, there is currently no prohibition on shares being sold by one spouse/civil partner on day 1 and 'repurchased' by the other spouse/civil partner on day 2.

6

Rents from Property

6.1 GENERAL

In general rent and other income receivable from the letting of land and buildings, less allowable expenses, is assessable to tax. This applies whether the letting is furnished or unfurnished, of a single room, or of a major block of buildings or area of land. The exception is the situation of mutual trading, as where rents are received from its members by a housing association not conducted for profit.

On and after 6 April 1995 all income from property in the UK, whether from furnished or unfurnished letting, is pooled and assessed as income from property. The computation will generally follow the rules applicable to trading profits, using standard accounting principles, but the income is regarded as investment income. Capital allowances continue to apply where applicable, including wear and tear allowances for furnished letting. Losses can be set off against pooled income and unrelieved losses can be carried forward. Income from overseas property will generally follow the above rules but will be assessable separately. Corporation tax on let property is unaffected.

6.2 UNFURNISHED AND FURNISHED LETTINGS

Rents received less certain expenses are taxable on a 'current year' basis. Payment of the tax is as for Self-Assessment: two payments on account and a balancing payment – the first is paid on 31 January in the tax year, the second on 31st July following the tax year, and the final balancing payment made the next 31 January. The payments on account are 50% (each) of the previous year's liability. Application may be made to reduce these payments if rents are falling, but interest payments may be made if the amount reduced is excessive. The net rents which are chargeable to tax may be those due under a weekly tenancy or even under a lease granted for hundreds of years.

The expenses which may be deducted for tax purposes from the rental income cover: maintenance and repair of the property, services provided, insurance, rates, rent payable, capital allowances or 10% wear and tear allowance on equipment provided and management expenses such as agent's commission for obtaining tenants and for rent collection. These expenses must have been incurred during the currency of the lease, so that expenses incurred before the landlord under assessment took over the premises cannot be charged. Capital expenditure, such as the cost of extensions and improvements to premises, is disallowed. See Chapter, Business Taxation, for details of the 100% relief for making available flats above commercial premises.

Capital allowances cannot be claimed on plant and machinery in a let dwelling house, but capital allowances may be claimed on plant and machinery used for the maintenance and management of the property. If the landlord occupies part of the premises let, the expenses must be apportioned on an equitable basis.

Example of a lettings computation:

	£	£
Rents receivable		20,000
Less: expenses:		
Water rates	3,000	
Maintenance of property	500	
Maintenance of furniture, etc.	250	
Insurance of furnishings	500	
Cleaning and other services	600	
Wear and tear allowance – normally at 10% of rent less water rates		
= 10% (20,000 – 3,000)	1,700	
		6,550
Taxable profit		13,450

Note: If only part of a house was let, the total council tax, water rates and other expenses would need apportioning on a reasonable basis, e.g. on floor space.

Where gross rents do not exceed £81,000, it is only necessary to submit to the Inspector of Taxes a statement showing gross income, total expenses and profit.

Losses may be carried forward to be set off against future profits, remembering that from 6 April 1995 all income from property is pooled.

Apportionments of premiums received for leases granted for 50 years or less are treated as rent in the year when the lease was granted. The basis of the calculation is the premium less one fiftieth for each year of the lease after the first year. For example, if a lease is granted for ten years at a premium of £2,000, the following amount is to be added to the rent in the first year:

	£
Premium	2,000
Less: £2,000 x (10 − 1) / 50	360
	1,640

A premium will be assumed where the tenant agrees to carry out work, or to make a payment in lieu of rent or as consideration for the surrender of the lease.

Business rents and connected persons. 'Connected persons' mean generally close relatives of individuals, and companies under common control. Where rent, such as for business premises, is paid between connected persons, it will, after 10 March 1992, be assessed on the recipient as it accrues, not when it is actually received. This applies to rent payable in arrears and when it is an allowable expense for business purposes. The object of the rule is to prevent deferment of tax by the recipient of the accruing income.

Short lets. It is not always appreciated that returns must be made to the Inspector of Taxes of profits from the occasional letting of rooms and that these profits are liable to tax. The consequence of a failure to make returns may be an estimated assessment going back many years, interest and possible penalties. (But see 6.4 below, Rent a Room Scheme.)

6.3 FURNISHED HOLIDAY LETTINGS

The beneficial tax treatment previously afforded to the letting of furnished holiday lettings (FHL) was to have ended on 5 April 2010 but the Coalition Government announced the Budget of june 2010 that the furnished holiday letting rules would **not** be withdrawn as from 6 April 2010. However, changes in the tax treatment of FHL were introduced in the 2011 Budget which came into effect from 1 April 2011 for companies and 6 April 2011 for individuals and partnerships:

- FHL in both the UK and European Economic Area will be eligible as qualifying FHL.
- The minimum period over which a qualifying property must be available for letting is increased from 140 days to 210 days in a year with effect from April 2012.
- The minimum period for which a qualifying property is actually let in a year is increased to 105 days from 70 days with effect from April 2012.
- Whereas losses from FHL could previously be offset against a taxpayer's other income, from April 2011 any such losses can only be carried forward for offset against profits from the same FHL business. There will be a

'period of grace' to allow businesses that don't continue to meet the criteria for days actually let to elect to continue to qualify throughout a period up to 2 years providing there is a genuine intention to meet the criteria.

As for other furnished lettings, the assessment was on the current year's profits and tax was payable in two instalments on 31 January in the year of assessment and the following 31 July. A loss could be carried forward or carried back for three years. Capital allowances may be claimed. Note that the rents may have been subject to VAT if they exceed £79,000 from 1 April 2013 (previously £77,000).

Hold-over relief for capital gains was available on disposal of the property.

The letting of caravans on a commercial basis is also normally assessable as trading income.

6.4   RENT A ROOM SCHEME

A relief was introduced from 1992/93 for individuals – owner occupiers and tenants – who let furnished accommodation in their only or main home.

Gross annual rents from this letting which do not exceed £4,250 in 2013/14 will be exempt from income tax altogether. Where the income exceeds £4,250, the person receiving the rent can either:

* pay tax on the amount by which the gross rent exceeds £4,250, without any further tax deduction for expenses, or
* pay tax on the profit (gross rents less actual expenses) in the normal way.

Where the rent is received jointly, such as in the case of a married couple sharing the income or by other than the resident, the limit of £4,250 is reduced by half to £2,125.

6.5   OVERSEAS PROPERTY

Rental income received by a UK resident from property abroad is subject to taxation in the UK. In many instances (consult HMRC for details) double taxation treaties will be in place with the relevant country, enabling UK residents to offset amounts already paid in local taxes abroad against their UK tax payable. Note, however, that if the foreign tax already paid exceeds the amount which would be charged under UK tax, no rebate will be offered by HMRC.

Note that capital gains tax will also be due in relation to any gains made by a UK-resident individual on the disposal of an overseas property, subject again to application of double-tax treaty offset provisions.

7

Miscellaneous Matters

7.1 ADDITIONAL ASSESSMENTS

Where the Inspector of Taxes discovers that there has been an undercharge to tax, the Revenue has the authority to make an additional assessment at any time up to five years from the filing date of the return.

If, however, there has been fraud or negligent conduct on the part of the taxpayer or a person acting on his or her behalf, the five-year limit is inoperative and additional assessments can be made for more than five years. A uniform time limit of 20 years applies for the recovery of tax in the case of default. But whatever the reason why income was not brought into charge earlier, assessments of this kind relating to income arising before the date of death cannot be made on the executors or administrators of a deceased person after the end of the third year following the year of assessment in which the person died.

Where the taxpayer has acted fraudulently, the Revenue authorities are permitted to impose penalties of varying sums as well as such additional assessments as may be appropriate. Failure to notify liability to tax can involve a penalty up to the amount of tax unpaid. In some instances the mitigation of penalties is allowed and, where that is so, the individual is invariably dealt with more leniently when he has voluntarily made a full and complete disclosure of the facts before their discovery by the Inspector. Penalty negotiations, particularly where large sums are involved, need to be handled with extreme care, and the assistance of an adviser well experienced in these negotiations is recommended.

7.2 CLUBS AND SOCIETIES

Many clubs, societies and other unincorporated associations are formed for the mutual benefit of the members and to provide communal services. These associations are generally considered to be 'companies' for taxation purposes and are therefore basically liable to corporation tax on trading, investment and letting income, as well as capital gains. Approved charitable associations are exempt, however, from tax. Many supplies used by charities are zero-rated for VAT.

The subscriptions and contributions payable by members are not normally taxable, nor are payments made by club members for goods and facilities which the club is set up to provide for them. On the basis that members' subscriptions and other receipts are applied to meet the running expenses of the club, they are not chargeable for the purpose of calculating the profit assessable for corporation tax.

Corporation tax will, however, be payable on the following:

- Activities which constitute trading, such as the holding of sales, sporting events, displays and the letting of club facilities for private purposes, and in these cases the applicable expenses can be set off against the income. However, tax will not normally be charged where the club makes it known that the profits from a particular event will be donated to charity and there is no regular trading or competition with other traders.

- Interest received, such as from bank deposits or from government or local authority stock, and including interest on national savings, but not dividends from UK companies. Where income tax is deducted from the interest, it can be set off against any corporation tax payable by the club, but the interest gross of income tax is chargeable in the corporation tax assessment. Building society interest must be grossed up for income tax by adding ¼ to the amount received and the income tax is likewise deductible from the gross corporation tax. Note that dividends received from UK companies are not chargeable to corporation tax and the tax credit on the dividend cannot be reclaimed.

For the financial year starting 1 April 2014, clubs and societies with profits chargeable to Corporation Tax of less than £300,000 will pay Corporation Tax at 20%.

In any event, provided they do not carry out competitive trading but apply surpluses to charities or club purposes, they should be able to avoid paying corporation tax, except on interest receivable.

7.3 THE COUNCIL TAX

The nature of the tax

In England, Scotland and Wales, the former Community Charge was replaced by the Council Tax from 1 April 1993. Domestic rates are still payable in Northern Ireland. Half the council tax consists of a personal element based on the residents in a dwelling, subject to the number of exceptions and reliefs;

the other half is a property element based on the value of the property, also subject to exemptions. Dwellings were valued at their saleable value on 1 April 1991 but there is provision for appeals against the valuations if made before the beginning of the council tax year.

In England, the valuations were placed in bands as follows:

Band	Values
A	up to £40,000
B	£40,001 to £52,000
C	£52,001 to £68,000
D	£68,001 to £88,000
E	£88,001 to £120,000
F	£120,001 to £160,000
G	£160,001 to £320,000
H	above £320,000

Different bands exist for properties in Scotland and Wales.

Exempt dwellings

Dwellings exempt from tax are those exclusively occupied by students and certain empty properties. Exempt properties are: those which have been empty and unfurnished for 6 months; those left empty by someone entering hospital, a nursing home or residential care home; those left empty as a result of the death of the occupier and pending probate or letters of administration; those left empty for 6 months due to structural alterations. The owner is liable for the tax if the property is empty but not exempt, or if it is not the sole or main residence of the owner, such as a holiday home.

The persons liable

The tax is payable by the resident of a dwelling and that person may be the owner, leaseholder or licensee of the premises. Joint owners are jointly responsible for the tax. If there are no residents of properties not exempt, only the property element (50%) is payable. With one resident the tax is reduced by 25%.

Traders and landlords are relieved from the proportion of the charge applicable to the trade or the letting.

Reliefs

The following people living in a dwelling do not count as residents for the purpose of the tax: persons under 18; students; apprentices and VTS trainees;

the severely impaired mentally. Residents who are disabled persons requiring extra space or rooms (such as downstairs bathrooms) are entitled to have the valuation of the premises placed in the next lower band, but there is no band lower than A. 80% of the tax is normally payable by persons receiving income support.

Payment by employer

Tax paid by an employer for an employee will be treated as a taxable benefit of the employee.

7.4   ERROR OR MISTAKE

It may happen that in completing his or her income tax return, the taxpayer makes a mistake which results in an excessive assessment. For example, an employed person may omit to claim the deduction of expenses wholly, exclusively and necessarily incurred in the performance of his duties; non-taxable capital receipts may have been included in business profits. Prior to 31 March 2010 relief could be claimed for tax paid in respect of excessive assessments arising through an error or mistake, and claims could be made within five years from the filing date of the return. Relief is not given where the excessive assessment was made according to the practice then generally prevailing. The *Finance Act 2009* introduced changes such that the time limit for claims made on or after 1 April 2010 is now 4 years from the filing date of the return (previously 5 Years).

A taxpayer, finding that he has inadvertently made a mistake in a return or other statement resulting in the under-payment of tax, should immediately disclose the fullest details to his Inspector of Taxes, since failure to do so may well make it difficult to refute a more serious charge in the event of the Revenue authorities discovering the matter for themselves.

However, from the introduction of self-assessment in 1997, the submission of an incorrect, incomplete or late return will lead to the imposition of an automatic penalty. The penalty is £100 plus interest on tax paid late and on the penalty itself! Another penalty is levied every 6 months.

The *Finance Act 2009* Finance bill introduced a new single penalty regime for incorrect returns for income tax, corporation tax, PAYE, NIC and VAT. Penalties will be determined by

- the amount of tax understated;
- the nature of the behaviour that gave rise to the understatement;
- the extent of disclosure by the taxpayer

It is possible to substantially reduce penalties where the taxpayer makes a disclosure, especially where this is unprompted, and there is a right of appeal against penalty decisions. The implementation of the new penalty regime is being phased in over a number of years starting in 2010/11 to allow time for the HMRC computer systems to be updated for the new rules.

7.5   INCOME FROM ABROAD

The tax rules generally

The essential tax rules, which have many qualifications, but largely depend on residential status or domicile (see below), are as follows:

- UK residents are liable for UK tax on income and capital gains whether arising in the UK or elsewhere.
- Non-residents are liable for UK tax on income arising in the UK but not on income arising outside the UK.
- Domicile affects inheritance tax. For individuals domiciled in the UK, inheritance tax is payable on assets wherever arising. Those not domiciled in the UK may incur liability to inheritance tax on UK assets.

The rules tend to be complex and, except in simple situations, merit expert advice.

Residence and domicile

Residence
The *Finance Act 2013* contained provisions for a new statutory residence test which came into effect from 6 April 2013. It will apply for income tax, capital gains tax, inheritance tax and corporation tax. It will not, however, be used to determine residence for national insurance purposes.

Under the new rules the concept of ordinary residence no longer applies from 6 April 2013 (subject to transitional provisions).

A detailed discussion of the new statutory residence test is beyond the scope of this book. What follows is a very brief introduction to the main provisions. The position for many individuals is likely to be very complicated and readers who think they may be affected by the rules are strongly advised to seek professional advice.

The statutory residence test is a three part test consisting of an automatic non-residence test, an automatic residence test and a sufficient ties test.

The basic rule is that an individual will be UK resident for a tax year where either the automatic residence test is met for the year or the sufficient ties test is met for the year.

An individual will satisfy the criteria of the automatic residence test if he meets at least one of the automatic UK tests and none of the automatic overseas tests.

The sufficient ties test is met for a tax year where an individual meets none of the automatic UK tests and none of the automatic overseas tests, but has sufficient UK ties during that tax year.

An individual cannot be UK resident if he meets any of the automatic overseas tests. For this reason the logical place to start when determining an individual's residence status is the automatic overseas tests then moving on to the automatic UK tests. Only if none of the automatic overseas tests and none of the automatic UK tests are met is there a need to consider the sufficient ties tests.

There are five automatic overseas tests, which are that an individual:

- was resident in the UK for one or more of the previous three tax years and is present in the UK for fewer than 16 days in the current tax year.
- was not resident in the UK for all of the previous three tax years and is present in the UK for fewer than 46 days in the current tax year.
- works 'sufficient hours' overseas with no significant breaks and spends less than 91 days in the UK of which less than 31 days count as 'working days' (more than three hours work).
- Dies in the UK having spent fewer than 46 days in the UK and was not resident in the UK in both of the previous two tax years.
- Dies in the UK and was in full time work overseas in the tax year of death.

There are four automatic UK tests which relate to time in the UK, a home in the UK, work in the UK and death:

- The first automatic UK test is that the individual spends at least 183 days in the UK in the tax year in question.
- The second test seeks to establish whether the taxpayer has a 'home' in the UK. This is satisfied if the individual has a home in the UK for all or part of the tax year, he is present at that home for a total of at least 30 days during the tax year and there is at least one period of 91 consecutive days which occurs whilst the individual has that UK home. At least 30 days out of that 91 day period must fall in the tax year under consideration. In addition, throughout the 91 day period the individual must either have no home overseas or else has one or more overseas homes but he is present there for a total of less than 30 days during the tax year. An individual is deemed to be present at a home if he is there at any point during a day, no matter how short the period of time.
- The third test concerns working in the UK and is satisfied where an individual works sufficient hours in the UK over a period of 365 days and part of this period falls into the tax year, has no significant beaks over more than 31 consecutive days from UK work and works for more than three hours in the UK for more than 75% of the working days (i.e. days on which

more than three hours work is performed).
- The fourth sufficient ties test is satisfied if an individual dies in the tax year, has a home in the UK and was UK resident for the previous three tax years.

The sufficient ties test links an individual's connecting factors to the UK with the number of days spent in the UK. The connecting factors are:

- Family members resident in the UK.
- Accommodation – the individual has accommodation in the UK and uses it during the tax year.
- The individual does at least 40 hours work in the UK during the tax year.
- The individual was present in the UK for more than 90 days in either or both of the previous two tax years.
- The individual spent more time in the UK during the tax year than any other country. This connecting factor is only considered in relation to individuals leaving the UK.

The application of the sufficient ties tests depends on the individual's previous UK residence. Essentially the greater the amount of time spent in the UK over the three preceding tax years, the less connecting factors are needed to pass the sufficient ties test and hence to be classified as UK resident for UK tax purposes.

Prior to 2013, ordinary residence generally meant living in the UK year after year on a permanent basis; but an individual who went abroad permanently could still be regarded as ordinarily resident in the UK if visits to the UK were made 183 days or more in a tax year, or for an average of 91 days or more in each tax year calculated on a maximum of 4 years. Ordinary residence (but not 'residence') could be retained by going abroad for a holiday lasting more than a tax year, and certainly for visits abroad for less than a year.

An individual was strictly a 'resident' in the UK if he or she lived in the country for any period, but there were a number of exemptions for short visits – see Section 7.8. In particular the status of being resident applied (a) for a stay of 183 days or more in a tax year; (b) on coming to the UK permanently; (c) on coming to the UK for at least 3 years; and (d) a stay in the UK for employment for at least 2 years.

For 2008/09 onwards, in deciding if an individual was resident in the UK for tax purposes, any day on which he was present in the UK at midnight was counted as a day of presence in the UK for residence purposes.

Domicile

A taxpayer's domicile is his or her natural and permanent home. It affects liability to inheritance tax and capital gains tax. A domicile of origin applies to an individual at birth and is that of the father, or the mother of an illegitimate child or one whose father has died. This may be changed to a domicile of choice on attaining 16 years of age. Certain dependent people may be incapable of choosing a domicile and will assume a domicile of dependency.

Crown employees are liable to UK tax wherever they may reside.

The Government has long expressed an intention to review the residence and domicile rules as they affect the taxation of individuals, and has (in April 2003) published a background paper for consultation.

Personal allowances

The general rule is that only individuals resident in the UK or Ireland are entitled to UK personal allowances. This rule is qualified by the fact that the following non-residents obtain full allowances:

- All citizens from European Economic Area (from 6 April 1996)
- Commonwealth citizens
- Crown employees, including civil servants and members of the armed forces, and their widows or widowers
- Employees of UK missionary societies
- Residents in the Isle of Man or Channel Islands
- Former residents in the UK who live abroad for health reasons and relatives who live with them
- Where a double taxation agreement allows a claim to the allowance.

Split year treatment

Under the law which operated before 6 April 2013, a taxpayer who was UK resident for part of a tax year was, strictly UK resident for the whole of the tax year. However, by concession, HMRC would split the tax year into resident and non-resident periods.

The new Statutory Residence Test (SRT) introduces new and more complex rules on this aspect. Under SRT taxpayers are either UK resident or non-UK resident for a full tax year and at all times in that tax year, but if during the year an individual either starts to live or work in the UK or starts to live or work overseas the tax year is split into two parts subject to meeting certain criteria:

- A UK part for which the individual is charged to tax as a UK resident, and:
- An overseas part for which the individual is charged to tax as a non-UK resident.

It is important to note that the split year treatment can only apply if an individual is UK resident for a tax year. This can give rise to situations where an individual would have been given split year treatment under the 'old' rules but no longer meets the criteria under the new tests if, for example, an individual comes to the UK to work towards the end of a tax year and is in the UK for less than 46 days during a tax year.

Non-residents – double taxation agreements

A person who is considered resident abroad is, in principle, liable to UK tax on income from the UK, but not on income from overseas sources. Such a person is also likely to be liable to the tax levied by the country of residence on his or her total income. Where, however, a double taxation agreement exists between the UK and the overseas country, double taxation is avoided by means of the following calculation:

(i)   Calculate the tax which would be payable on the UK income alone, after deducting applicable UK allowances from that income.

(ii)   Calculate the UK tax which would be payable on the total income, UK as well as overseas income, after deducting UK allowances from that total income. Multiply the UK tax so calculated by the fraction:

$$\frac{\text{UK income}}{\text{Total income}}$$

(iii)   The UK tax payable is the greater of the amounts arrived at in (i) and (ii) above and, unless the UK income is very large, will normally be the result of the second calculation.

Non-residents – tax-free interest

A further relief to non-residents is that they can arrange for interest on certain UK government stocks to be paid to them without deduction of UK tax; or if the tax has been deducted to claim repayment from the Inspector of Foreign Dividends. The stock in question includes: Exchequer Bonds, Funding Loan, Savings Bonds, Victory Bonds and 3½% War Stock.

Foreign employment income

The taxation of employment income is largely dependent on where the employment duties are performed. As a general rule, if an employee performs his or her duties within the UK, earnings in respect of those duties will be taxed in the UK at the time they are received. This is the case regardless of the residence and domicile status of the employee.

Where an employee performs duties outside the UK earnings in relation to those duties will be taxed on a receipts basis or a remittance basis depending on the employee's residence and domicile situation.

Where earnings are taxed on a receipts basis the date of receipt is generally the earlier of the time when payment is physically made or the time when the employee becomes entitled to the payment.

The remittance basis refers to the amount of earnings that are brought back or enjoyed in the UK. Significant changes have been made to the remittance basis of taxation with effect from 2008/09.

The rules can be summarised as follows:

Status in the UK	UK duties	Overseas duties
Resident	Receipts basis	Receipts basis
Resident & non-domiciled	Receipts basis	Receipts basis *
Non-resident	Receipts basis	Not taxable

* Except if working for a foreign employer wholly outside the UK, in which case the remittance basis applies.

In normal circumstances the expense of travelling to an employee's normal place of work is not an allowable expense. There is, however, a special relief for foreign travelling expenses.

The special rules apply to employees who are resident and ordinarily resident in the UK who incur travelling expenses to take up a foreign employment. Such travelling expenses are deductible in calculating the employee's net taxable earnings. A deduction is also allowed for travel expenses on the completion of the overseas duties.

The amount of allowable expenses includes expenses in relation to the employee's spouse and children under the age of 18. A deduction is allowed for two outward and two return journeys in any tax year.

There are similar provisions in respect of non-domiciled employees' expenses of travelling to take up an employment in the UK.

Changes to the remittance basis

For 2008/09 onwards, if a non-domiciled or not ordinarily resident person aged over 18 has been UK resident in more than 7 out of the last 10 years he will only be able to use the remittance basis for that tax year if he pays an additional charge of £30,000. In the 2011 Budget the Government announced that a higher £50,000 annual charge for individuals who have been UK resident for more than 12 years and who claim the remittance basis. This will take effect from April 2012.

The charge will not apply in cases where the individual's unremitted foreign income and capital gains for the tax year is less than £2,000.

Where such a taxpayer elects not to pay the £30,000/£50,000 charge, he will be taxed on his worldwide income and gains.

The £30,000/£50,000 charge will be collected through the self-assessment system.

UK residents using the remittance basis for any tax year will not be entitled to UK personal reliefs or the capital gains annual exemption.

Foreign business interests

Where a UK-resident is entitled to income from a foreign business, such as a holiday property company registered offshore, he or she will normally be assessable to UK tax on the whole of the income arising from that business. Registered foreign companies will normally be subject to corporation tax in the country of registration, although HMRC will take a careful look at where the company is being managed (if it is managed from the UK it may be liable to UK Corporation Tax). For sole traders or partnerships operating abroad the assessment will normally be on the profits for the accounting period ending in the current tax year (as is the case with UK-based unincorporated businesses).

Pensions from overseas sources

Where a UK resident receives a pension from overseas sources, and the British government has assumed responsibility for the payment, the whole amount of the pension is assessable, not just the amount remitted to the UK. However, a deduction of 1/10th of the pension is allowed, or the whole of it for a pension payable for victims of National Socialist (Nazi) persecution in Germany or Austria.

Withholding tax

UK resident taxpayers who receive foreign income from which foreign tax has been deducted may be able to obtain relief from double taxation. This is normally achieved by claiming foreign tax credit relief in the taxpayer's self-assessment tax return. It is also possible to make a claim to deduct the foreign tax when calculating the amount of income chargeable to UK tax. Taxpayers must choose one method or the other. They cannot do both. The amount of foreign tax credit relief is subject to the overriding principle that it cannot exceed the UK tax on the same item of income.

7.6 INTEREST ON TAX

Interest on repayments

Interest, called a 'repayment supplement', is payable by the Inland Revenue in the case of a repayment of income tax or capital gains tax. If the repayment results from excess interim payments on account, interest will run from the actual dates the excess payments were received (i.e. usually around 31 January in the tax year and the following 31 July). To the extent the repayment results from an error in the balancing payment made on the 31 January following the tax year concerned, interest will run from this date as well.

Interest is also due on a repayment to a company of corporation tax, tax credits or investment income, or tax suffered by deduction. In this case the repayment is made after the end of 12 months from the latest date when the corporation tax was payable on the company's profits. The individual company must be resident in the UK. The interest is not taxable.

Interest on tax overdue

Subject to some special exceptions, interest is chargeable on tax unpaid. Historically interest below £30 was not charged but the use of computers now allows the increased ability to charge for all late payments of tax. The interest is not an allowable expense for tax purposes.

7.7 DISCRETIONARY AND ACCUMULATION TRUSTS

In 2010/11 the trust rate of tax was increased to 42.5% on dividend income and 50% on all other income. These rates were reduced to 37.5% and 45% respectively from 6 April 2013.

The rate applicable to trusts applies to:

- the income of discretionary and accumulation trusts other than dividends
- the capital gains of all trusts and estates of deceased persons in administration, and
- certain amounts received by all trusts (e.g. gains from offshore funds).

When a beneficiary receives a payment of income from the trust he or she is treated as if the income had already been taxed at the trust rate. If the beneficiary's overall level of income for the year was such that they were liable for tax at lower rates, they may be able to reclaim some or all of the tax suffered on the trust income.

From 6 April 1995 the rules applicable to the taxation of trust income were simplified such that:

- If the settlor or the settlor's spouse has retained an interest in the trust, the income is treated as that of the settlor for tax purposes.
- The income is also treated as that of the settlor where the trust or settlement is in favour of the settlor's minor unmarried child.
- Where the settlor or the settlor's spouse receives a loan from the trustees, or makes a loan to them, the settlor is liable to income tax on the annual value of the loan, by reference to a statutory rate of interest.

7.8 VISITORS TO THE UK

Individuals covered

This section gives a general guide to the position of foreign-domiciled nationals who stay in the UK for substantial periods and receive income here. It also applies to British nationals when they return to the UK after long periods abroad, having meanwhile lost their UK residential status. The subject tends to be specialised and in a complicated situation expert advice is desirable.

Residence

The crucial question is whether the visitor is considered to have become resident in the UK. The general rules covering residence in the UK are as. The general rules covering residence in the UK from 6 April 2013 are as outlined in section 7.5 above.

UK tax liability

- **Non-residents.** No UK tax is payable on income, e.g. pay, arising overseas. Income arising in the UK is, however, liable for UK tax at the basic rate and no personal allowances can be obtained.

- **Residents.** Individuals becoming resident here are liable for UK tax and are entitled to full personal allowances for the tax year in which they arrive.

7.9 STAMP DUTY

Some kinds of transfers are subject to Stamp Duty, such as the transfers of shares, transfers of property and certain instruments such as declarations of trust. From 30 November 2001, stamp duty exemption is available for the purchase of property in certain designated disadvantaged areas of the UK, and where the consideration or premium for a lease does not exceed £150,000.

The current rates are set out in the following table:

Stamp Duty land Tax Rates from 22 March 2012

1. Transfers of property (consideration paid)

Rate	Disadvantaged areas		All other UK property	
	Residential	Non-residential	Residential	Non-residential
0%	£0-150,000	£0-150,000	£0-125,000	£0-150,000
1%	£150,001-250,000	£150,001-250,000	£125,001-250,000	£150,001-250,000
3%	£250,001-500,000	£250,001-500,000	£250,001-500,000	£250,001-500,000
4%	£500,001-1,000,000	£500,000+	£500,001-1,000,000	£500,000+
5%	£1,000,001-2,000,000	n/a	£1,000,001-2,000,000	n/a
7%	£2,000,000+	n/a	£2,000,000+	n/a

2. New leases (lease duty)

Rate	Net present value of rent	
	Residential	Non-residential
0%	£0-125,000	£0-150,000
1%	£125,000+	£150,000+

8

Value Added Tax

8.1 THE GENERAL NATURE OF THE TAX

VAT came into effect for transactions made on and after 1 April 1973 and replaced purchase tax and the selective employment tax. The legislation is contained in the *Value Added Tax Act 1994*, as amended by the subsequent Finance Acts, and detailed provisions set out in numerous statutory orders issued from time to time.

The rate for most taxable goods and services not zero-rated was increased to 20% from 4 January 2011 (previously 17.5%). Increasingly, a 5% band is being expanded, including fuel and power for domestic or charity use, installation of energy-saving materials, children's car seats, certain residential conversions, and, from 1 July 2006, all sales of contraceptives.

VAT is a common method of indirect taxation in the European Union and, subject to variations of treatment amongst the member States, is made obligatory by a Directive of the Council of the EU. In the UK it takes the form of a charge on the invoiced value of applicable goods and services made by traders who are not exempt. The amount so charged to customers may be set against the VAT suffered by the trader on his or her purchases; in some cases this calculation may lead to a repayment of tax to the trader. The tax suffered by a business on its purchases is called 'input tax' and that which it charges its customers is called the 'output tax'.

The system operates right through the chain of importation or production of goods, through the distribution via wholesalers, until the final sale from the retailer to the consumer. It is thus the ultimate consumer who bears the tax on the sale price of purchases. As will be seen from the example below, the tax eventually takes the form of a tax on value added to basic raw materials or services.

Some goods and services are 'exempt' from the tax, and this means that the trader will not be able to charge the tax on sales to customers nor be able to obtain a credit for 'input tax' on relevant purchases. Exemption from all goods sold also applies to traders with a turnover of no more than £81,000 from 1 April 2014 (£79,000 previously) but exemption may not be an advantage since, although they cannot charge their customers with the tax, they are unable to claim credit for input tax suffered.

Many categories of goods and services are 'zero-rated'. This also means that the trader dealing in such goods cannot charge customers with the tax but can claim credit for relevant input tax.

8.2 THE SYSTEM ILLUSTRATED

Assuming that the goods are taxable and not zero-rated, and that the traders concerned are not exempt but are 'registered' with the Customs and Excise, the system, in its simplest form, may be illustrated as follows:

		£	£
1.	A manufacturer buys raw materials at a basic price of	1,000	
	on which his supplier charges VAT at 20%, i.e.	200	
		1,200	
2.	The manufacture sells to a wholesaler goods	2,000	
	produced from the raw materials at a basic price of		
	to which he adds VAT of	400	
	the wholesaler paying	2,400	
3.	The manufacturer pays to the Customs and Excise:		
	VAT on his invoice	400	
	Less: VAT on his purchase	200	
			200
4.	The wholesaler sells the goods to a retailer at	2,800	
	plus VAT	560	
	the retailer paying	3,360	
5.	The wholesaler pays to the Customs and Excise:		
	VAT on his invoice	560	
	Less: VAT on his purchase	400	
			160
6.	The retailer sells to the consumer at	4,200	
	plus VAT	840	
	the consumer paying	5,040	
7.	The retailer pays to the Customs and Excise:		
	VAT on his sale	840	
	Less: VAT on his purchases	560	
			280
			640

This £640 represents 20% on the value added to the raw material, i.e. 20% of (£4,200–£1,000).

8.3 TAXABLE SUPPLIES

VAT is payable only where there is a taxable supply, i.e. the goods or services are those covered by the tax and are not exempt or zero-rated. VAT is payable on imports of taxable goods as though it were a customs duty, and it may be payable by a UK agent who is working on commission for an overseas principal.

Goods produced by a business or acquired by a business and used for the purposes of that business, e.g. stationery printed in the business, are taxable at market value. This is the process known for VAT purposes as 'self supply'. Where, however, goods are produced by a business or acquired by a business and applied by the owner for personal use, the cost of those goods is taxable. Cost is not defined for this purpose but, in the case of manufactured articles, it is thought to mean direct cost, e.g. materials and labour, plus manufacturing overheads.

Samples and promotional gifts are taxable at the cost to the supplier but if that cost is no more than £50, from 6 April 2001 (previously £15), they will be tax free. VAT can be recovered on the cost of gifts over the limit if they are accompanied by a certificate indicating that output tax will be accounted for. Industrial samples for testing and market research are also tax free, whatever their cost or value, provided they are not of the kind obtainable in the market place.

Goods supplied on hire purchase are taxable on their cash price, i.e. excluding interest or hire purchase charges, which are not subject to VAT.

Goods and services will be taxed net of cash discount, provided the rate is shown on the invoice and whether or not the discount is taken by the customer.

For retailers using the cash basis, VAT is paid on cash received, so that bad debts are automatically relieved of the tax. With the alternative basis, VAT is paid on credit sales invoiced plus cash sales.

8.4 THE TAX POINT

This is the point when liability to the tax arises, although the actual payment or repayment of tax may not be due until some months later. Basically the tax point is when the goods are despatched or made available to the customer, but the tax point may be extended to the date when the invoice is issued within 14 days of the despatch of the goods. The Commissioners are authorised to agree special arrangements as to the tax point with particular traders.

In the case of goods on sale or return, the tax point is when the goods have finally been accepted by the customer, but this date must not be more than 12 months after despatch to the customer.

In the case of goods on hire (not hire purchase or credit sale) the tax point is when each successive payment becomes due, and such point may be expressed in the agreement, or when an invoice is issued, if earlier.

For goods on hire purchase the tax point is when the goods are supplied.

8.5 ADMINISTRATION

Registration

A trader is obliged to register for VAT with the Customs and Excise where turnover exceeds £81,000 from 1 April 2014 (previously £79,000). On registration, the trader must show on the invoices issued the tax added to the relevant charges, except in the case of retailers making cash sales; and must make normally quarterly returns, paying or reclaiming the difference between input and output tax. It could, however, be advantageous to register, even though turnover is expected to be below the limit, where input tax was likely to be more than output tax and the difference could be reclaimed. Registration can be cancelled where turnover is below the limit of £79,000 from 1 April 2014 (previously £77,000).

In the 2011 Budget the Government announced that it will require online VAT registration, deregistration and notification of changes from 1 August 2012. The Government also require all remaining VAT registered persons to file their VAT returns online and pay electronically from 1 April 2012.

Records and tax invoices

All traders who are not exempt are obliged to keep records of their purchases and sales including records of the VAT applicable on those transactions. They are also obliged to keep what is called a 'tax account' in which their total liabilities or claims in respect of VAT are recorded. No particular form of record or account is specified. The authorities have the right to inspect records (including computer operations) and tax invoices and may obtain the power to enter premises for this purpose. Special regulations apply to the records of retailers.

All non-exempt traders, except retailers making cash sales, must issue what are called 'tax invoices' on making sales. A tax invoice is simply an ordinary invoice which contains certain specified information, i.e. the usual invoice details plus: the number of the invoice, the registered number of the supplier, the type of supply (e.g. whether zero-rated, etc.) and the tax charged. Exempt and zero-rated supplies must be separated even though they are included in one invoice with taxable goods. Invoices need not be issued for zero-rated supplies, second-hand goods relieved of tax, gifts, and goods for which input tax is not deducted.

Returns and payments

Returns showing the input and output tax for the period must normally be submitted to the Customs and Excise at specified three-monthly intervals, and these claims will show the amount of tax to be paid or repaid. Where the business is likely to obtain a repayment, application may be made for the returns and the settlement to be made monthly, thus helping to improve the cash flow of the business. From 1 April 2006, businesses with a turnover below £1,350,000 (previously £660,000) can opt for annual accounting subject to nine estimated payments in advance, with a tenth adjusting payment.

If returns are not made or they are inaccurate, the authorities may make an estimated assessment on the trader. Such an assessment must be made within six years after the end of the accounting period concerned but cannot be made after three years from the death of the trader. The trader may appeal against an assessment to the Commissioners and thence to a quasi-judicial body, independent of the Commissioners, known as a VAT tribunal.

Flat rate scheme for smaller businesses

The flat rate scheme is intended to be a simplification measure that allows businesses to calculate their net tax due by applying a flat rate percentage to their inclusive total turnover (i.e. including all reduced, zero-rated and exempt income). The scheme applies to certain trade sectors only.

The scheme is open to small businesses with an annual taxable income (excluding VAT) not exceeding £150,000. Businesses must leave the scheme if either their VAT inclusive turnover exceeds £230,000 calculated by reference to any anniversary of the start date, or if the business VAT inclusive turnover in the next 30 days can be expected to exceed £230,000 alone.

Penalties

Penalties, fines and interest may be payable for failure to comply with the VAT legislation. In the case of failure to pay the amount due the authorities have the ultimate power of obtaining a distress warrant with a view to the sale of the taxpayer's goods, furniture and other chattels.

A unified penalty regime is being introduced in respect of the failure to make or deliver returns or documents on or before the filing deadline for the return in question. The new regime replaces the current array of penalties and treats late filing and late payments separately. As regards VAT the new system of penalties came into force with effect from 1 April 2009 although the old system will apply to periods ending before that date.

The amount of penalty payable under the new regime is geared towards the amount of extra tax payable as a result of the incorrect return and whether the error in the return was as a result of lack of care on the part of the taxpayer or deliberate and (possibly) concealed. No penalty is payable if the taxpayer can demonstrate that he took reasonable care in preparing the return. Penalties are also lower where the taxpayer notifies HMRC of the error without being prompted. The table below summarises the situation in relation to the late filing of VAT returns.

Penalty rates for inaccurate VAT returns

Reason for the error	Disclosure of the error to HMRC*	Minimum penalty (as % of the tax)	Maximum penalty (as % of the tax)
Careless			
(i.e. you fail to take reasonable care)	Unprompted	0%	30%
	Prompted	15%	30%
Deliberate			
(i.e. you knowingly sned HMRC an incorrect document)	Unprompted	20%	70%
	Prompted	35%	70%
Deliberate and concealed			
(i.e. you knowingly sned HMRC an incorrect document and try to conceal the inaccuracy)	Uprompted	30%	100%
	Prompted	50%	100%

A disclosure is unprompted if at the time you tell HMRC about it you have no reason to believe they have discovered it, or are about to discover it.

From 11 March 1992 a penalty was not normally imposed unless the net VAT under-declared or overpaid exceeded £2,000 in an accounting period. For accounting periods commencing on or after 1 July 2008 the £2,000 *de minimis* limit was increased to the greater of £10,000 or 1 per cent of turnover, subject to an upper limit of £50,000. Errors below these *de minimus* limits can be corrected by the taxpayer on the next VAT return after the error is discovered. Errors greater than £10,000 or 1% of turnover escape a penalty (but not interest) if they amount to less than 30% of the gross amount of tax (GAT) i.e. 30% of the combined value of the output and input tax figures that should have been stated on the return.

A default surcharge applies to late returns and late payments on three occasions, the maximum penalty being 15%. Reliefs are available for small businesses with annual turnover of less than £150,000 in relation to the penalties for late payment of tax.

Cash accounting

Registered persons must inform the Customs and Excise for VAT to be based on the amounts paid and received during a quarterly or monthly accounting period. This system can simplify the accounting requirements for many of the smaller businesses and, where substantial credit is given to customers, improve the cash flow. Bad debts are automatically accounted for by failure to receive the amount due.

Two significant changes to the rules for reclaiming VAT on bad debts were included in the *Finance Act 2002*.

- A business claiming bad debt relief is no longer required to send a written notice to the debtor.
- A business that has claimed input tax on a supply but has not paid the supplier within six months of the supply (or payment due date, if later) must repay the input tax to Customs and Excise.

It could be a disadvantage in terms of cash flow when tax receivable on purchases is higher than tax payable on sales and where long terms of credit are taken on supplies.

Cash accounting is available where turnover is not expected to exceed £1,350,000 in the year from 1 April 2007 (previously £660,000), and can continue until turnover reaches £1,600,000 (previously 825,000). The VAT outstanding must not exceed £5,000. It operates from the beginning of the normal tax period for the business and must be continued for at least two years. Transactions excluded from a cash accounting system are: imports, exports, hire purchase, conditional and credit sales.

Tax invoices must continue to be kept and, for cash (not cheque) payments, they need to be receipted. Receipts and payments by credit card are entered at the date of the invoice, but giro transactions, standing orders and direct debits at the date of entry in the bank account. Part payments or receipts should be related to specific invoices.

8.6 EXEMPT TRADERS

These are (a) small traders with a turnover of no more than £81,000 from 1 April 2014 (previously £79,000), and (b) traders who deal only with exempt supplies. The first category need not register, do not have to charge VAT on their sales, and are not liable to account for VAT, but they cannot recover from the Customs and Excise the VAT charged on their purchases. They can register voluntarily and if they do so they are no longer exempt. The second category of trader cannot obtain refunds of input tax, but where there are both taxable and exempt supplies a proportion of the input tax is refundable.

8.7 EXEMPT GOODS AND SERVICES

A large number of kinds of goods and services are exempt from VAT – that is to say, VAT cannot be charged when such goods are sold, even by a registered trader. These categories are summarised below.

Group 1 The grant of any interest in or right over land but not the letting of accommodation, parking or camping facilities or fishing or taking game. Bedroom accommodation in hotels is taxable but not other accommodation in hotels, or elsewhere. From 1 August 1989 an election (subject to many qualifications) can be made to waive this exemption, and thus recover input tax.

Group 2 Insurance, covering also services provided by brokers and agents; but most marine, aviation and transport insurance is zero-rated. Note that insurance premium tax was imposed from 1 October 1994 (currently 5%).

Group 3 Postal services, but not cable services.

Group 4 Betting, gaming and lotteries, but admission charges, club subscriptions and takings from gaming machines are taxable.

Group 5 Finance, i.e. dealing in money or credit, banking and the sale of securities, but stockbrokers' commissions and unit trust management fees are taxable. The charge made by credit card companies on retailers is exempt. Where banks buy in credit card processing, the charge for this service is not exempt.

Group 6 Education, including the supply of incidental services and covering the facilities provided by youth clubs and similar organisations.

Group 7 Health, covering goods and services provided by medical practitioners, dentists, opticians (the eye test is exempt, as is carrying out the resulting prescription, but the provision of spectacles is not (from 1 July 2001, the standard VAT rate will be charged on the total cost), nurses, pharmaceutical chemists, hearing aid dispensers, hospitals, etc. Protective boots and helmets purchased by businesses are chargeable.

Group 8 Burial and cremation services.

Group 9 Trade unions and professional bodies.

Group 10   Sports competitions and physical education.

Group 11   Works of art, etc. Disposals exempt from capital gains tax. (See also under Section 8.9.)

Group 12   Fundraising by charities.

Group 13   Cultural services, etc.

8.8   ZERO-RATED SUPPLIES

Zero-rating means that, although the goods are theoretically taxable, the rate of tax is nil. Because zero-rated goods are taxable, suppliers of these goods can recover tax they have suffered on relevant purchases; they do not, however, charge tax on their sales of zero-rated goods. All goods exported by a registered trader are zero-rated, but not goods exported or imported for processing and re-exported or re-imported. Other zero-rated supplies are set out in Schedule 8 *VAT Act 1994,* subsequent statutory orders, and the *Finance Act 1989*, and these groups are summarised below.

Group 1   Food for human consumption, including many packaged goods, animal feeding stuffs, but not soft drinks (it has now been held that freshly-pressed citrus fruits are zero-rated), alcoholic drinks, confectionery, ice-cream, petfoods, seeds, and animals yielding food for human consumption. There are many exemptions to the above.

Group 2   Water, other than distilled water, and sewerage services except when supplied to businesses from 1 July 1990.

Group 3   Publications such as books, newspapers, periodicals, music, maps, etc., but not stationery.

Group 4   Talking books, radio sets, boats, maintenance of 'talking books', recorders and magnetic tape and radio sets for use by the blind and handicapped. From 1 April 1986 much other equipment for handicapped persons or charities was zero-rated, including lifts, alarms and welfare vehicles; from 1 April 1989 medical sterilising equipment for charities; and from 1 April 1992 toilet facilities in charitable buildings.

Group 5   Construction of dwellings or residential accommodation, or property for charitable purposes, and the grant of a major interest in the property, including sale of the freehold or grant of lease for over 21 years, but only when the trader is the person constructing the building. Residential accommodation includes homes for children, the aged and infirm, students, the armed forces, monasteries and nunneries. In accordance with EU law the construction of new industrial and commercial buildings will be subject to VAT for contracts made after 1 April 1989. The letting for one or two weeks in a year of time-share holiday homes by a long lease is not zero-rated (*Cottage Holiday Assoc. Ltd. v Customs and Excise, 1982*). Note that land is exempt and that the maintenance of buildings is chargeable at the VAT rate. VAT also applies to structural alterations, sheds and greenhouses in private gardens, and fixtures in new buildings, but not to substantial conversion, alteration and enlargement of ancient monuments and listed buildings. However, zero-rating is applied to building alterations for the benefit of a resident handicapped person. Landlords can opt to charge VAT on non-residential rents. In this case tenants pay tax on half the rents in the first year, or for five years where they are charities.

Group 6   Protected buildings

Group 7   Services to overseas traders or for overseas purposes.

Group 8   Transport, covering the supply, services and maintenance of ships above 15 tons and not used for recreational purposes; and aircraft above 18,000 pounds and not used for recreation; and the transport of passengers in vehicles carrying 12 or more passengers (i.e. excluding taxis). Airline meals are not taxable.

Group 9   Caravans above the limits for use as trailers (i.e. 22.9 feet in length or 7.5 feet in width) and houseboats.

Group 10   Gold bullion and gold coins, when supplied by a Central Bank to another Central Bank or to and from a Central Bank to a member of the London Gold Market. The *Finance Act 1993* s45 provides that on and after 1 April 1993 where any person makes a supply of gold for business purposes that supply is a taxable supply, but not a zero-rated supply. Where the supplier is a taxable person and the supplies are made in connection with the business of the customer, the latter (i.e. the purchaser) must account for and pay tax on the supply on the supplier's behalf. The supplies may consist of gold, gold coins and goods containing gold, taxable at the open market value of the gold contained in the goods.

Group 11   Bank notes.

Group 12   Drugs, medicines and appliances supplied on prescription, whether under the National Health Service or otherwise including ambulances and wheelchairs supplied to hospitals and car adaptations for the disabled; cars leased to disabled persons under mobility schemes; medical and scientific equipment, including computers, donated to hospitals; bathroom equipment for the handicapped in charitable residential homes, and equipment for charitable first aid and rescue services.

Group 13   Imports and exports subject to qualifications.

Group 14   Tax-free shops.

Group 15   Charities. Much equipment used or supplied by charities is zero-rated (see also under Group 4) and zero-rating is applied to medicinal products supplied to a charity for medical research, both for humans and animals – see Value Added Tax (Handicapped Persons and Charities Order) 1986 – and also to charities' television, radio and cinema advertising, donated goods, and equipment for veterinary research.

Group 16   Clothing for young children, industrial safety clothing and motor cycle crash helmets.

Also zero-rated from 1 April 1993 are protective boots and helmets and parts and equipment for certain ships and aircraft not used for recreation.

8.9   THE LOWER 5% RATE

VAT on domestic fuel was reduced to 5% in 1997. The subsequent Finance Acts have extended the 5% band to include:

(a) Domestic energy-saving materials – the supply and installation of energy-saving materials such as insulation, draught stripping, hot water and central heating system controls, as well as solar panels, to all homes. This was introduced from 1 April 2000 but does not apply to the DIY market. However, from 1 June 2002, the 5% VAT rate is applied to the domestic installation of grant-funded heating equipment
(b) Women's sanitary products (from 1 January 2001)
(c) Children's car seats from (11 May 2000)
(d) Certain residential conversions and renovation of dwellings (from 11 May 2000).

(e) Air source heat pumps and micro combined heat and power units (from 7 April 2005)

(f) Supplies of advice or information relating to the welfare of the elderly or disabled, and children

(g) All sales of contraceptives (from 1 July 2006).

(h) Smoking cessation products other than those already zero-rated as a result of being dispensed on prescription. The reduced rate will only apply for a period of one year from a date subject to parliamentary approval but originally expected to be 1 July 2007. The 2008 budget contained an announcement that secondary legislation would be laid before Parliament will extend this relief for an unspecified period.

(i) Alterations to housing for elderly people with effect from 1 July 2007.

8.10 MISCELLANEOUS

- **Business entertainment.** Tax suffered on business entertaining cannot be deducted from output tax. Tax on allowable subsistence for business purposes is, however, deductible from output tax.

- **Hotel accommodation, catering and tourism.** Up to four weeks accommodation, including board and service, is taxable at the current VAT rate. After four weeks, the charge for the rent of the room or rooms is not taxable. The charge for the use of services will be assumed to be not less than 20% of the accommodation charge excluding meals. The charge for meals will also bear the current rate. Gross profits by tour operators on tours in the European Union are taxable.

- **Second-hand Goods.** The 'margin scheme' of VAT applies to all second-hand goods, works of art, antiques and collectors' items but not to precious metals and gem stones. The margin scheme requires VAT to be accounted for on a net basis on sale of the goods – i.e. both purchase tax and sales tax are accounted for at the same time, at the point of sale.

8.11 MOTOR CARS

VAT

VAT is charged by the seller on the price charged to the buyer and is reclaimable by a dealer whose business it is to sell cars, and by companies buying their own cars wholly for business use.

Reclaiming VAT

An individual or company buying a car for use in the business, or for private use, cannot reclaim the tax which it has paid to the dealer or on importing the car, unless it is acquired new for re-sale or for use in, or lease to, taxi firms, self-drive hire firms and driving schools, subject to adjustment for personal use.

Vehicles chargeable to VAT

These are essentially private type cars for use on public roads and constructed or adapted for carrying passengers. Vehicles not chargeable are those accommodating only one, or more than twelve, passengers; of above 3 tonnes unladen weight; caravans, ambulances, prison vans, approved taxi cabs; and special vehicles not for carrying passengers, such as ice-cream vans, mobile shops and offices, hearses and bullion vans. VAT is payable when an exempt vehicle is converted to carry passengers. Cars used by manufacturers for research and development are relieved from VAT. Exemption is also extended to cars leased to handicapped persons, and to members of visiting forces and to individuals with diplomatic privileges.

Leasing and hire purchase

VAT must be paid on the sale price when a car is acquired by hire purchase and can be reclaimed by a dealer. If a car is leased VAT must be charged on the rentals and can be reclaimed by the lessor if in business, but only 50% where any use of the car is made for private motoring. Vehicles purchased for leasing to the disabled are relieved from car. (See also under 'Reclaiming VAT' above.) No refunds of VAT can be claimed where businesses buy company cars on long leases from EU suppliers who do not conduct business in the UK.

Repairs and maintenance

VAT is chargeable on the cost and can be reclaimed in full by a business even if there is some private use.

Sale of used cars

Basically VAT must be charged on the sale price of used cars, whether sold by a dealer or by a business using the car for the business. However, the special scheme applicable to such sales enables the VAT to be charged only on the excess of the selling price over the purchase price of the car. No tax invoice is issued and the input tax cannot be reclaimed.

Fuel benefit

This is the scale charge for income tax on fuel provided free or below cost to employees for their private mileage.

Car fuel scale rates

This Revenue and Customs Brief announced changes to the VAT fuel scale charge. These changes take effect on 1 May 2011 and businesses must use the new scales from the start of their first accounting period beginning on or after this date. The existing VAT fuel scale charge, which is based on the engine size and fuel type of a car, is replaced by a fuel scale charge based solely on the CO_2 rating of a car. The new table, which mirrors that used for direct tax purposes is reproduced below.

CO_2 Emissions Figure	12-month return Scale charge	VAT due per vehicle	3-month return Scale charge	VAT due per vehicle	1-month return Scale charge	VAT due per vehicle
	£	£	£	£	£	£
120 or less	627.00	104.50	156.00	26.00	52.00	8.67
125	939.00	156.50	234.00	39.00	78.00	13.00
130	1,004.00	167.33	251.00	41.83	83.00	13.83
135	1,064.00	177.33	266.00	44.33	88.00	14.67
140	1,129.00	188.17	282.00	47.00	94.00	15.67
145	1,190.00	198.33	297.00	49.50	99.00	16.50
150	1,255.00	209.17	313.00	52.17	104.00	17.33
155	1,315.00	219.17	328.00	54.67	109.00	18.17
160	1,381.00	230.17	345.00	57.50	115.00	19.17
165	1,441.00	240.17	360.00	60.00	120.00	20.00
170	1,506.00	251.00	376.00	62.67	125.00	20.83
175	1,567.00	261.17	391.00	65.17	130.00	22.67
180	1,632.00	272.00	408.00	68.00	136.00	22.67
185	1,692.00	282.00	423.00	70.50	141.00	23.50
190	1,757.00	293.83	439.00	73.17	146.00	31.67
195	1,818.00	303.00	454.00	75.67	151.00	25.17
200	1,883.00	313.83	470.00	78.33	156.00	26.00
205	1,943.00	323.83	486.00	80.83	161.00	26.83
210	2,008.00	334.67	502.00	83.67	167.00	27.83
215	2,069.00	344.83	517.00	86.17	172.00	28.67
220	2,134.00	355.67	533.00	88.93	177.00	29.50
225+	2,194.00	365.67	548.00	91.33	182.00	30.33

Where VAT is reclaimed on fuel used for private purposes VAT according to scale is added to the output tax. It may not be beneficial to reclaim VAT on fuel if the amount so claimed is less than the scale charge.

8.12 RETAILERS

Retailers are not obliged to prepare tax invoices unless they are demanded by customers, and hence a number of special schemes for accounting for VAT are available for retailers and are set out in Notice 727 issued by the Customs and Excise.

8.13 BAD DEBTS

Normally, where a supplier has suffered a bad debt incurred by an insolvent customer, the supplier can reclaim VAT he has already paid on the supplies concerned. The sale must have been at open-market value and the title in the goods must have passed. The supplier must prove in the bankruptcy, or liquidation in the case of a limited company, for the debt less the VAT.

As mentioned above (Section 8.5 Administration – Cash accounting) two significant changes to the rules for reclaiming VAT on bad debts were introduced in the Finance Act 2002:

- A business claiming bad debt relief can no longer be required to send a written notice to the debtor.
- A business that has claimed input tax on a supply but has not paid the supplier within six months of the supply (or payment due date, if later) must repay the input tax to Customs and Excise.

By the exercise of an option for cash accounting, where turnover is below £1,350,000, bad debts will be automatically relieved from VAT. VAT can be reclaimed on bad debts which are more than six months old based on date of supply (previously one year old) and have been written off in the trader's accounts. Relief for bad debts is available for barter transactions; the relief can be back-dated to when the debt arose. A three-year limit is to be put on the age of the bad debt.

8.14 DIRECTORS' ACCOMMODATION

VAT is not recoverable on costs, such as repairs, incurred on accommodation provided by companies for directors or their families.

8.15   TREATMENT FOR INCOME AND CORPORATION TAX

Persons exempt from VAT

Allowable business expenses can include VAT charged on purchases, etc.

Other persons

Income and expenditure is to be brought into the tax computation exclusive of VAT.

8.16   SINGLE EUROPEAN MARKET

From 1 January 1993, border controls between members of the European Union (EU) were largely abolished.

Before 1 January 1993 controls of imports and exports were carried out by Customs and Exercise at the frontiers. As a result the exporter had to claim customs clearance for zero-rating on the shipment of goods and for imports before the goods were released by customs.

From 1 January 1993 VAT is charged, if applicable, not on the importation of goods but on the acquisition from other EU states. The tax point of 'acquisition' is the 15th of the month following acquisition, or the date of the invoice. Where goods pass from an EU state to a non-EU state, controls at the border will remain. To obtain zero-rating of exports, the supplier must show on his invoice not only his UK VAT registration number but also that of his customer in the importing state, and submit to the Customs a quarterly list of such exports.

Where customers are not VAT-registered sales up to various limits (depending on the EU state concerned) are chargeable to VAT. Above these limits VAT is payable in the importing state and this may involve appointing a VAT representative in that state.

The members of the EU, with effect from 1 May 2004, were the UK, Austria, Finland, Sweden, Germany, France, Italy, Spain, Belgium, Portugal, Denmark, Greece, Ireland, Luxembourg, the Netherlands, Cyprus*, Czech Republic, Estonia, Hungary, Latvia, Lithuania, Malta, Poland, Slovakia and Slovenia.

Bulgaria and Romania became full members of the EU with effect from 1 January 2007. Croatia became a full member of the EU with effect from 1 July 2013.

*The European Commission has advised that, although the entire island of Cyprus joined the EU on 1 May 2004, the application of EU law will be suspended in those areas of Cyprus in which the Government of the Republic of Cyprus does not exercise effective control.

9

Inheritance Tax

9.1 GENERAL NATURE OF THE TAX

Inheritance Tax may arise on the amount of a taxpayer's wealth passing on death, on certain lifetime transfers and on certain transfers into and out of trusts. The tax applies when the total value of the estate and the chargeable transfers exceeds £325,000 in 2014/15 and 2013/14 for deaths and the rate is 40%. Subject to the many exemptions indicated below, the amount chargeable to the tax includes the value of property both in and outside the UK where the deceased was domiciled in the UK; but only property in the UK is valued for those domiciled elsewhere, although in such cases double taxation relief may apply.

The *Finance Act 1986* gave the new title of 'inheritance tax' to what was previously called 'capital transfer tax'. The latter tax was not repealed but was substantially amended, particularly by the elimination of tax on most lifetime gifts. The amended provisions apply to deaths after 17 March 1986 and gifts or transfers made after that date.

The following sections cover only the essentials of inheritance tax, which represents a very complex body of legislation. For more detailed information it will be necessary to obtain expert professional advice.

For a more detailed explanation of Inheritance Tax and estate planning generally, readers are referred to the book *Inheritance Tax Simplified*, also published by Management Books 2000.

9.2 EXEMPTIONS

- Property passing on death and within the seven years prior to death up to a value of £325,000 in 2013/14 and 2012/13).
- Transfers or gifts between spouses or civil partners made on death or at any time previously. Prior to 6 April 2013, transfers between spouses or civil partners were subject to a limit of £55,000 if the recipient was domiciled abroad. Following criticism from the European Commission that the capping of the spouse exemption is discriminatory, the *Finance Act 2013* will contain provisions which increase the level of the cap to the

level of the nil-rate band (currently £325,000). From 6 April 2013 non-UK domiciled transferee spouses or civil partners will also be able to elect into UK domicile for the purposes of the spouse exemption. The election can be made by the non-UK domiciled spouse during the lifetimes of both spouses or after the death of the UK-domiciled spouse.

- Gifts which represent normal expenditure out of income.
- Lifetime gifts in consideration of (i.e. before) marriage: those by the parents of the married couple up to £5,000; by a remoter ancestor up to £2,500; and by others up to £1,000.
- Gifts to charities, for national purposes and the national benefit; also gifts to political parties.
- Cash options to widows and dependents under approved annuity schemes and certain overseas pensions.
- Tax-free government securities in the beneficial ownership of persons not domiciled or ordinarily resident in the UK; and all property outside the UK owned by such persons.
- Gifts for the maintenance or education of a spouse or civil partner, child or dependant.
- Majority holdings of shares given to employees on trust.
- Legacies disclaimed within two years of death.
- Lifetime transfers up to £3,000 a year, this limit excluding the small gifts exemption of £250 a year.
- Bona fide transfers of property in the course of trade for adequate consideration and allowable for income tax.
- Where death was attributable to injury or disease arising from active service with the armed forces.
- Certain gifts made more than seven years prior to death – but note that these gifts may trigger a capital gains tax liability on the giver. See 9.6 Potentially Exempt Transfers (PET).

9.3 THE VALUE TRANSFERRED

Where a specific sum of money is given, either on death or during lifetime, the value transferred is the amount of money in question. In the case of transfers of other assets, such as investments, jewellery, furniture, land and buildings, the asset will need to be valued at market value at the date of transfer. More strictly the value to be taken into account is the loss in value to the donor.

Transfers of shares in unquoted companies made within seven years before death (except to a wife) should be made at a freely negotiated price, so that no chargeable benefit arises.

The gross value of the estate at death may include interests in applicable trusts, such as discretionary trusts and sums due to the estate, such as under life policies and death benefit under pension schemes. From the gross value of the estate deductions are made for debts, including income tax due at death, and funeral expenses, but not executorship expenses.

Other lifetime transfers that are not potentially exempt transfers (see below) are chargeable at half the full rate. Where death occurs within 7 years prior to death the balance of the full rate becomes payable, subject to tapering relief (see below).

9.4   GIFTS WITHIN SEVEN YEARS PRIOR TO DEATH

Gifts made within the seven years prior to death will be chargeable to the appropriate rate of inheritance tax, subject to 'tapering relief' – see below.

9.5   TAPERING RELIEF

The tax payable on chargeable gifts or transfers made within three to seven years of death is reduced or 'tapered' according to the following scale:

Period before death	Proportion of tax payable
6 to 7 years	20%
5 to 6 years	40%
4 to 5 years	60%
3 to 4 years	80%
up to 3 years	full rate

9.6   POTENTIALLY EXEMPT TRANSFERS (PET)

These are transfers which will only become chargeable if death occurs within seven years after they are made. Prior to 22 March 2006 they included gifts to individuals and accumulation and maintenance trusts set up for members of the deceased's family or for the disabled. They did not include transfers into discretionary settlements which were immediately chargeable lifetime transfers.

After 22 March 2006, however, gifts to all trusts except trusts for disabled persons are classed as immediately chargeable lifetime transfers.

Where a PET becomes a chargeable transfer because of death, the tax payable on it is determined by any gifts made in the 7 years prior to that gift. This means that any gift made in the 14 years before death will either incur a direct liability (within 7 years of death) or increase the liability on a gift inside the 7-year period (if such a gift is made within 7 years of the first gift).

9.7   GIFTS WITH RESERVATION

These are gifts made after 17 March 1986 with a reservation for the donor to obtain a benefit. Examples of reservations would be the retention of a right to obtain income or enjoy the gifted property, to continue to live in a gifted house, inheritance trusts and insurance policies for the mitigation of the tax.

A gift with reservations to an individual will be taxed on the death of the donor, but one made to a trust or company will be taxed when it is made. Tax will be charged on the gift when the reservation is released, or the enjoyment of the property ceases, e.g. on the death of the donor, subject to credit for any tax already paid. Exceptions include the case where reasonable provision is made for a relative who becomes unable to maintain himself or herself after the gift was made.

Pre-owned Assets Tax

The Government introduced this new income tax by way of the *Finance Act 2004*. The charge is intended to apply where Inheritance tax-saving arrangements have been made by which a person gives away assets but continues to use or enjoy those assets.

Broadly, pre-owned assets are assets which were at one time owned by a chargeable person but which have been disposed of wholly or in part since March 1986. The legislation has introduced separate rules which set out what counts as enjoyment of assets and how to calculate the tax charge in respect of land, items of personal property and intangible assets (for example, shares or insurance policies).

The tax came into effect from 6 April 2005 but it is important to understand that it will be imposed in respect of schemes or arrangements set up before the tax was announced – back as far as March 1986.

Where the tax applies, it will be charged as if the chargeable person's income was increased by the deemed value of the benefit received. For example, if the asset given away was property with a market rental value of £25,000 per annum, then the chargeable person would be treated as though his income was increased by £25,000 and he will be taxed at his highest marginal rates, even though he has not received any such income.

There are some exemptions built into the legislation and taxpayers can opt, if they wish to avoid the tax, to accept that the assets given away will be treated as if they still form part of their estate for Inheritance Tax purposes only.

9.8   OTHER RELIEFS

The more important other reliefs are as follows:

Business Property Relief

Where a transfer of value includes relevant business property, the value transferred is reduced by a percentage (currently either 100% or 50%). This is known as business property relief (BPR).

BPR does not have to be claimed, it is given automatically. It is given in respect of lifetime tax, death tax and tax on trusts.

For transfers on and after 10 March 1992 and any recalculation of tax on earlier transfers following a death on or after that date, the relief is given at the following rates.

Relevant business property

	Percentage Reduction	
	10.3.92 to 5.4.96	**6.4.96 to present**
A business carried on by a sole trader	100%	100%
An interest in a business, e.g. partnership	100%	100%
Transfer out of shares in or securities of a company which is listed and held by a controlling shareholder	50%	50%
Transfer out of shares in or securities of company which is not listed and held by a controlling shareholder	100%	100%
Transfer out of a substantial minority shareholding (i.e. >25%) in an unlisted company	50%	100%
Land, buildings, machinery or plant owned by an individual and used by a company he controls/ his partnership	50%	50%
Land, buildings, machinery or plant owned by a settlement	50% or 100%*	50% or 100%*

* Assets held by a trust can only qualify for BPR if:

    (a) they are used for the purposes of a business carried on by a person with a qualifying interest in possession in the trust that owns the assets; and

    (b) that business comprises relevant business property.

100% BPR is available on the transfer of the trust assets if the business in which those assets are used is transferred at the same time. Only 50% BPR is available in situations where there is a transfer of trust assets but the business itself is not transferred but retained by the person with the interest in possession.

An interest in possession in settled property exists where the person having the interest has an immediate entitlement to any income produced by that property as the income arises.

Agricultural land

100% relief from inheritance tax is available, subject to conditions, for agricultural land passing after 10 March 1992 (previously 50%). The main conditions are:

- That the property was occupied by the deceased (or transferor) for the purpose of agriculture throughout the period of two years before death or transfer;
- That the property was owned by the deceased (or transferor) for seven years before death (or transfer) and occupied for that purpose by the deceased (or transferor) or by another person;
- The relief applies to leases of agricultural land at full market value, and is available for farmland subject to agricultural tenancies acquired as a result of the death of the previous tenant. The death must have occurred on or after 1 September 1995;
- In all other cases the relief is at 50%;
- Relief is also available for land dedicated to wildlife habitats.

Quick succession relief

This is a scaled reduction of the tax payable on death where the deceased received chargeable transfers within five years before death. The tax is reduced by 80% where the transfer was made two years before death, 60% for three years, 40% for four years and 20% for five years.

Property sales

Where sales of freehold or leasehold property are made within 4 years after death (previously 3 years), the sale price may be substituted for the value at death for inheritance tax purposes.

9.9   RE-ARRANGEMENT OF ESTATES

Within two years after death the dispositions of an estate made by a will can be rearranged by the written agreement of all beneficiaries, and this could have the effect of reducing inheritance tax. These rearrangements will only be effective for inheritance tax purposes where they make adequate provision for the dependents of the deceased.

9.10   GENERAL CONCLUSIONS

The foregoing is no more than a résumé of the essentials of this highly complex tax. Expert professional advice is of the greatest importance when taxpayers seek to mitigate this tax. Subject to proper advice, the tax can be relieved by such methods as: taking advantage of the annual exemptions for gifts, transfers to spouses and to charities, and the establishment of trusts for children and dependents. If the risk of dying within seven years is accepted, substantial gifts during lifetime instead of legacies at death may be appropriate.

Note to readers

- Every effort has been made to ensure that the advice given in this book is correct, but the publishers, authors, editors and consultants regret they cannot accept any liability whatever for errors of omission or commission arising from the use of these notes. The publisher is not in the business of giving legal or financial advice or other professional services.

- Your Tax Return must be based on the official forms sent to you by the Inland Revenue, and their Official Guides and Help Sheets, or via the official documentation available on the internet.

- There is a great deal of useful information (albeit in government-speak) on the Inland Revenue website at www.hmrc.gov.uk. There you will find explanations for the various rates of taxation, and tables with current figures for a whole range of taxes, as well as the facility to make your tax return online.

- If you feel that your tax affairs are more complicated than you can manage yourself, you are strongly advised to seek the help from a professional tax adviser. That is far better than getting it wrong and invoking the wrath of the Inland Revenue, or even more serious, having to pay more tax than you need, because you didn't have the guidance you really needed.

Index

A

Accommodation 44
Adopted children 30
Allowance
  first-year 80
  initial 80
  writing down 80
Annual investment allowance (AIA) 79
Authors, artists and entertainers 96
Averaging profits
  artists 96
  farmers 97

B

Bad debts 144
Balancing allowances 84
Balancing charges 84
Barristers 98
Bed-and-breakfasting 111
Benefits 37, 40
Blind persons 30
Business
  expenses 45
  loans 45, 51
Business cars 41, 84
Business computation 39
Business entertainment 141
Business Property Relief 150

C

Capital allowances 77
  annual investment allowance (AIA) 79
  enhanced 87
Capital gains
  business 90
Capital Gains Tax (CGT) 22
  bed-and-breakfasting 111
  exceptions 101
  gifts 109
  hold-over relief 110
  indexation 103
  losses 106
  on death 108
  overseas property 115
  private house 108
  reinvestment in EIS 110
  rollover relief 107
  spouses and civil partners 109
  taper relief 103
  trusts 106
Carry forward 89
Cars 41, 84
  CO2 emissions 41, 78
  fuel scale charges 42
  fuel scale rates 143
  leased 85
  VAT 141
Cars, business 41
Cessation 88
Charitable gifts 44, 50
Child allowance 30
Child benefits 30
Child care 30
Children 30
Children's Bonds 60
Child Tax Credit 31
Child Trust Fund 35
Civil partners 36, 109
Close companies 57, 94
Clubs and societies 116
Company cars 41, 84
Complaints 14
Construction industry 98
Corporation tax 22, 90
Council tax 117
Customs and Excise duties 23

D

Deep gain securities 58
Directors' accommodation 144
Direct taxes 21
Divers 97
Dividends 57
Domicile 120, 122

E

Employee share schemes 63
Enterprise Investment Scheme (EIS) 65, 110
Enterprise Management Incentive Scheme 64
Errors or mistakes 119
Expenses 45
  allowable 71
  disallowed 70

F

Farmers 97
First-year allowances 80
Foreign business interests 126
Foreign employment 124
Foreign income 120
Foreign pensions 126
Friendly societies 61
Furnished lettings 112

G

Gifts 44, 109, 148
Gifts with reservation 149
Gratuities 44

H

Hire purchase 86
HM Revenue & Customs (HMRC) 20
Hold-over relief 110
Holiday lettings 114
Home 108
Home-working 46

Husband and wife 35

I

Income
  assessable 73
  not assessable 73
Income disregard 32
Income from abroad 120
Income tax 21, 55
Incorporated businesses 70
Indexation 103
Indirect taxes 23
Individual Savings Account (ISA) 61
Inheritance tax 22
  exemptions 146
  gifts with reservation 149
  tapering relief 148
Inheritance Tax 152
  agricultural land 151
  business property relief (BPR) 150
  potentially exempt transfers (PET) 148
  property sales 151
  quick succession relief 151
Initial allowances 80
Interest
  accrued 58
  on tax overdue 127
  overseas 57
  receivable 59
  taxed 57
  untaxed 57
Investment companies 94
Investment trusts 66

J

Job finder's grant 49
Job seeker's allowance (JSA) 49
Junior ISAs 61

L

Lettings 112
Life assurance 47

Limited companies 90
Living abroad 120
Loans 51
Losses
  carry-back 89
  relief 89
Loss of employment 39

M

Married couple's allowance 29
Medical insurance 46
Ministers of religion 98
Money laundering 21

N

National Crimes Agency (NCA) 21
National Insurance 23, 48
National Savings 60

O

Occupational sick pay (OSP) 49
Offshore funds 67
Overseas income 120
Overseas property 115

P

Parties 44
Partners
  change of 88
Partnerships 69
Pay as you earn (PAYE) 37
Pensions 55
  from abroad 126
Personal allowance 28
Personal Equity Plan (PEP) 58
Personal taxation 55
Plant and machinery
  energy efficient 86
  leased 85
Potentially exempt transfers (PET)
  148
Premium Bonds 60
Pre-owned Assets Tax 149

Private house 108
Property
  abroad 115
  rents from 115
  sale of 108

R

Rates and the Council Tax 23
Reliefs and allowances 28
Relocation 45
Rent-a-room scheme 115
Rents from properties 115
Replaced plant 85
Residence
  country of 120
  visitors 128
Rollover relief 107

S

Save as You Earn 60
Savings income 67
  starting rate 22, 56
SAYE share option scheme 62
Scholarships 30
Scrip dividends 66
Season tickets 46
Security assets 86
Self-assessment 13, 16, 17, 25
Self-employed 95
Share incentive plans 64
Share options 62
Social security 48
Split year treatment 123
Spouses 109
Statutory Maternity Pay (SMP) 46
Statutory sick pay (SSP) 49
Strikes 49
Subcontractors 98

T

Taper relief 103
Tax
  codes 38

credits 30
direct 21
indirect 23
returns 13
schedules 23
system 23
Trusts 127

U

Unemployment 39, 49
Unfurnished lettings 112
Unincorporated businesses 69, 88
Unit trusts 66
Universal credit 31

V

Value Added Tax (VAT) 23, 145
    bad debts 144
    cars 141
    cash accounting 136
    European Union 145
    exempt goods and services 137
    exempt traders 136
    flat rate scheme 134
    lower rate (5%) 140

margin scheme 141
penalties 134
persons exempt 145
retailers 144
second-hand goods 141
taxable supplies 132
zero-rated supplies 138
Venture Capital Trusts (VCT) 66
Visitors to the UK 128

W

Widow's bereavement allowance 30
Withholding tax 126
Woodlands 98
Writing-down allowances 80